C000138256

HOW TO PREPARE FOR A CAREER IN

FASHION

STEPHANIE FINNAN

Published by
Adelita Ltd
www.adelita.co.uk

This edition published 2011
Copyright © 2011 Stephanie Finnan

Author: Stephanie Finnan
Designer: Lee Mitchell
Publisher: Jenny Ross
Cover Illustration: Julie Bouiguerourene www.jwls.fr

ISBN: 978-0-9552017-5-2

Printed and bound in Finland

How to Prepare for a Career in Fashion is an easy-to-follow guide that provides you with advice on all aspects of how to enter this exciting yet competitive industry. Inside, you'll discover how to prepare for your career in fashion – with tips on what you should be doing now and on how to stay one step ahead of everyone else!

If you're still at school, at college or university, or even looking to transfer into fashion from another industry, this is the book for you. There are 11 chapters, each covering a different role in fashion, and they contain everything you need to know about the most popular jobs, including:

A JOB PROFILE

Featuring what's involved in each sector, from the day-to-day responsibilities and what to expect for a salary and for the working hours, to related roles.

ESSENTIAL INFORMATION

Including the skills you need for the job, an outline of qualifications and courses to consider, and a list of the best and worst things about working in each role.

INTERVIEWS

Featuring interviews with industry insiders from all of your favourite stores and brands, including Topshop, AllSaints, River Island and ASOS, plus luxury companies such as Lulu Guinness, Liberty of London and Versus for Versace. These people give you all the inside info on what it's really like to work in fashion – the highs, the lows, the perks – and, more importantly, how they got to where they are now.

ASK THE EXPERT

Including answers to all your most popular careers questions, based on real queries that were sent to me from students at schools and colleges across the UK. Has your question been featured? Read on to find out...

All of this, plus lots of advice on education, college/university courses and how to find work experience, ensures that you'll be as prepared as possible to enter the industry.

I decided to write this book following the Clothes Show Live at Birmingham in 2009. On the stall for my careers advice company, The Fashion Careers Clinic, I was inundated with requests for guidance on everything from college course information to the low-down on what roles are available in fashion. It soon became clear that there is a real need for honest, practical advice for people who are considering a career in fashion, but don't know how to go about it. Therefore I've tried to include as many of your queries and topics as possible, and I hope you find this guide useful. Please let me know what you think – you never know, your query might be included in the next guide. Email me at: steph@fashioncareersclinic.com

Good luck with preparing for your career in fashion!

Steph X

CONTENTS

TOP: Sholto Drumlanrig
MIDDLE: Andy Thompson
BOTTOM: Alice Jackman, c/o Topshop

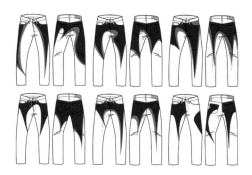

TOP: Photo: Gemma Booth/Stylist: Mhairi Gibb
MIDDLE: MUA: Claire Salter/Photographer: Robert Harper
BOTTOM: Mohsin Sajid (C) LEVI'S JAPAN K.K / OKI-NI LTD

Considering a career in fashion is an exciting prospect, but it can be confusing deciding on your route into the industry. We've answered a couple of the most common questions students sent to us, relating to education and general career concerns. You're likely to have many more queries about fashion education – more than we have space for here, unfortunately. However, the good news is that there's lots of information available online about fashion courses and training – go to the end of this chapter for a list of useful websites.

I WOULD LOVE TO WORK IN THE FASHION INDUSTRY BUT IN TODAY'S CLIMATE IS THIS A REALISTIC CAREER PATH TO CHOOSE?

It's as realistic as going into any other sector. While the fashion industry has been affected by the recession in recent years, it still accounts for the employment of approximately 120,000 people throughout the UK.

To give yourself a head start in terms of career prospects, it's worth considering the less obvious job choices instead of focusing on the very popular sectors of womenswear fashion design, buying or PR. So many people leave college or uni wanting to find work in these sectors where there are more graduates than there are jobs.

However, there are certain roles available in the industry that aren't chosen so often, as they are seen as being less glamorous, such as pattern cutting and production. These sectors are relatively understaffed, and employers are keen for more graduates to train in these areas. You will probably find that, if you leave college/uni with production or technology-based skills, you will find a job more quickly than someone who has trained in design, for instance.

DO YOU HAVE TO BE GOOD AT ART TO PURSUE A FASHION CAREER?

No, although it clearly helps if you want to go down the design route. However, there are lots of jobs in fashion that don't require good art skills. Only a small percentage of people work in the design sector – there are many more working in the technical and business side of the industry, who have skills in subjects such as Sewing, Maths, English and languages.

IS HAVING A PART-TIME JOB IN RETAIL USEFUL?

Yes, experience working in fashion retail can definitely help increase your understanding of the industry. Try to secure a role with a fashion retailer you feel would enhance your CV in your future career. For instance, if you eventually want to be a fashion designer for a big name luxury brand, it makes sense to begin working in a designer clothing store if possible. This will give you a better understanding of quality fabrics and unusual pattern-cutting/fabrication techniques, as well as broadening your customer awareness.

While working in a retail role, take the opportunity to assist in other areas of the business and ask to help out doing visual merchandising, personal styling and buying if possible – all these things will look great on your CV.

IS THE FASHION INDUSTRY AS COMPETITIVE AS IT SOUNDS?

Yes, as the people interviewed in this book explain, fashion is very competitive. You should be prepared to work hard and be enthusiastic about what you do, and really love all aspects of fashion – you won't be successful in this industry if you're half-hearted about it.

IS THERE ANY FUNDING AVAILABLE FOR PEOPLE WHO NEED HELP WITH PAYING FOR TRAINING OR COURSE MATERIALS?

The Prince's Trust offers Development Awards of up to £500 for residents of the UK. This money can be used for training courses (although not to pay university fees), course materials such as books and specialist equipment, and for travel costs/childcare while training. To be eligible for the award, you must be aged 14–25. For full criteria and an application form, take a look at their website or call 0800 842842 for more information.
www.princes-trust.org.uk

You might be eligible for Education Maintenance Allowance (EMA) if your household income is £30,810 or less. This is paid on a weekly basis, in sums of £10, £20 or £30, depending on your circumstances. You will have to meet certain criteria,

including the following:
- You need to be 16, 17 or 18 and to have left — or be about to leave — compulsory education.

You need to be enrolled on:
- a full-time further education course at a college or school; or
- a diploma funded by the Young People's Learning Agency (where available); or
- a course that leads to an apprenticeship
- For further information, look at the Education and Learning section here: www.direct.gov.uk

ARE THERE ANY FASHION-RELATED COURSES AROUND FOR TEENAGERS?

If you aren't yet at the stage of being ready for university or full-time college, there are some good short courses and summer schools available for teenagers in textiles, portfolio presentation, styling and sewing — in fact, whatever route you want to go down, there should be a course suitable for you. Check the websites of your local colleges, libraries and art & craft centres to see what they have to offer.

DO YOU HAVE TO DO UNI COURSES TO GET A GOOD JOB IN FASHION OR CAN YOU JUST LEAVE THE SIXTH FORM AND TRY AND WORK YOUR WAY UP?

It depends on the type of role you want. While there are certainly a few careers you can get into without going to university (including sales, styling, make-up, visual merchandising and pattern cutting), most companies ask for candidates who have a degree. The fashion industry is so competitive that without one you may find it difficult to get into the more popular jobs such as fashion, textiles and accessories design or buying, where most people are educated to BA degree level. Employers often don't have the time or resources to train people from scratch, so are looking for people who've already been trained in the basics while at uni or college.

I'M REALLY INTERESTED IN FASHION DESIGN BUT I DON'T KNOW WHAT TO TAKE FOR MY A-LEVELS (HIGHERS, IN SCOTLAND) IN ORDER TO ACHIEVE THIS.

As universities and higher education colleges will ask you to present a portfolio of work at interview, it makes sense to take art in the sixth form to help you prepare for this. Other good options include textiles and perhaps a language, which might come in useful later in your career. Some schools offer a fashion/textiles A-level — if yours doesn't, it might be worth transferring to another sixth form that does if you particularly want to take this option. It doesn't matter too much what else you take at A-level, as long as you can show evidence of strong portfolio work and a flair for fashion later on if applying for uni or college.

WHAT GRADES SHOULD I AIM FOR?

To get on to a foundation, GNVQ or diploma course you will need at least 4 GCSE grades at C and above.

After university, it's not all about the grades you achieve — although it's obviously good to aim high, there are people who have gained a first at degree level who haven't landed a job, and also people who got a third in their degree but have found work. Getting on in the fashion industry is more about your personality, making contacts and, for the more creative roles, how good your portfolio is.

I'M NOT SURE WHICH AREA OF FASHION I WANT TO GO INTO. I'M RELYING ON DECIDING WHAT WORKS BEST FOR ME WHILE AT UNIVERSITY OR WHEN I START WORK. IS THIS A GOOD IDEA, OR SHOULD I HAVE A CLEARER PLAN?

It's perfectly OK to be undecided at this stage. In fact it's better to be open-minded and not restrict yourself — you never know what might appeal once you've been at uni for a few years. When choosing a

Image: Julie Bouiguerourene

university course it's best to go for a general fashion course, as each module gives you a taster of each aspect of the industry, including design, pattern cutting, textiles and graphics, styling, sewing and trend research.

Also go for a uni course that offers curriculum time spent on work placement — the longer the better — giving you the opportunity to explore a couple of different roles to enable you to discover what you prefer doing and where your skills are. Some people are adamant that they want to be a designer, but then find that they're better at the technical elements of fashion such as pattern cutting.

Completing your final project during your last year of uni will give you the chance to specialise in a certain area, in preparation for deciding what to do when you graduate. Even if you're undecided after university, you can still do a couple of work placements following graduation to help you make your mind up — there's no rule that says you must make a decision to go down a certain path immediately.

WHICH COLLEGES/UNIVERSITIES ARE CONSIDERED THE BEST TO STUDY AT, ACCORDING TO EMPLOYERS IN THE INDUSTRY?

While a select number of companies look out for candidates who studied at 'big name' universities (such as the London College of Fashion or Central St Martin's), the majority of employers are more interested in you as an individual, rather than the particular uni you went to. If you impress them at interview and have the correct skills for the job, they won't be checking your CV for this information.

However, there are certain universities that are particularly respected in the industry for their specialist courses, such as Cordwainers College in London, which is well known for its comprehensive courses in accessories design, and De Montfort University in Leicester which offers a BA degree in Contour Fashion, covering training in lingerie, underwear and performance sportswear.

WOULD I BE BETTER STUDYING A-LEVEL/HIGHERS TEXTILES/FASHION OR DOING A DIPLOMA OR FOUNDATION COURSE AFTER HIGH SCHOOL?

This depends on whether you are certain that fashion is the right career choice for you. If you're pretty sure that fashion is what you really want to do, it might be worth going straight on to a college foundation or diploma course, where you are likely to get more practical training. Also, because the majority of foundation and diploma courses are offered at higher education colleges, you will have the opportunity of training and learning in a more mature environment than at school or sixth form.

If you aren't entirely sure about fashion, and wavering between other options, then A-levels/Highers might be a better route for you. This will give you the opportunity to study several other subjects alongside fashion/textiles, giving you the flexibility to go down other career routes or study something else at university if you decide that fashion isn't for you after all.

WHAT IS THE BEST ROUTE INTO FASHION – IS IT UNIVERSITY OR ARE THERE WORK-BASED COURSES INSTEAD?

This completely depends on which area of fashion you want to get into. For some sectors you don't have to go to uni at all (although there are specialist courses for nearly all fashion subjects). However, if you're keen to gain a qualification, there are several routes you can take, from short courses and evening classes to longer-term options.

If you aren't sure that a traditional university course such as a BA degree is right for you, there are more practical courses available in the form of foundation degrees. This type of course offers the opportunity to spend the majority of your time actually working in the industry with a local business, while also studying at college, and is similar in some ways to an apprenticeship. The bonus with this type of course is that, while you still get a qualification at the end of it, you also gain real skills and training in a specialist sector and often the opportunity to gain employment with your mentor company at the end of your course.

I'M LEAVING SCHOOL IN A YEAR AND KNOW I WOULD REALLY LOVE TO DO SOMETHING LIKE FASHON OR TEXTILES, BUT I DONT KNOW WHAT COURSES ARE AVAILABLE OR WHERE I SHOULD START LOOKING.

After high school there are lots of different routes you can take and it can be a bit confusing deciding which one to opt for. Take a look at the following pages to see what types of course are available and which might be the best for you.

Once you've established what sort to go for, you can begin searching to find all the relevant courses in your area. There are thousands to choose from – we've listed a couple of options in each chapter, but these are just a tiny fraction of what's available, so you will have to do your own extensive research to find the most suitable ones for you. The easiest way to do this is by looking online – we've listed some of the main websites that show courses available throughout the UK at the end of this chapter.

Please note that all of the educational information on the next few pages is written from a UK perspective, for students looking to study in England, Northern Ireland, Scotland or Wales.

All images: Julie Bouiguerourene

Not sure what options are available to you once you've left high school? There are thousands of routes you could take, from part-time courses, apprenticeships, further education at college, certificates in your chosen subject, then university. This chart gives a brief overview of the most popular ways to gain skills and training for your entry into the fashion industry, however it is by no means an exhaustive list of options.

At the time of writing this book, many changes are taking place within the education sector, particularly in relation to the renaming of National Diplomas. With this in mind, I highly recommend that all students check with their chosen education institution as to the courses available, and also check online via the websites listed on the final page of this chapter.

TYPE OF STUDY	QUALIFICATION	LENGTH	FURTHER INFO
FURTHER EDUCATION	A-LEVELS / SCOTTISH HIGHERS	1–2 YEARS	These courses can be completed as a route into higher education and many students go straight from A-levels/Highers to a specialist fashion degree. This type of study is suitable if you enjoy the academic side (ie, writing, research and analysis of a subject). It can be useful to take these qualifications if you aren't 100% sure if you want to do fashion, as they will give you a good route into doing other subjects at uni if you later decide that fashion isn't for you.
FURTHER EDUCATION	GNVQ OR SVQ / FOUNDATION IN ART & DESIGN	1–2 YEARS	Either of these qualifications are good preparation for entry to higher education. You will study a variety of art & design disciplines and may have the opportunity to specialise in fashion or textiles in the latter part of the course.
FURTHER EDUCATION	NATIONAL DIPLOMA IN ART & DESIGN OR FASHION	2 YEARS	This course is a work-related (vocational) further education option. It is designed to provide training in practical skills and give an overview of the industry, such as basic sewing and pattern cutting and portfolio development.

TYPE OF STUDY	QUALIFICATION	LENGTH	FURTHER INFO
HIGHER EDUCATION	HIGHER NATIONAL DIPLOMA or CERTIFICATE IN FASHION	2 YEARS	Students get the opportunity to study at a more advanced level on these courses, broadening their understanding of the industry, and developing more complex skills. Some graduates may progress straight into industry after gaining these qualifications. However, this is rarer than it used to be, with most graduates progressing to university where they are admitted to the final year of a BA course and will gain a degree qualification following successful completion of the course.
HIGHER EDUCATION	FOUNDATION DEGREE	2 YEARS	These courses are equivalent to two years of an honours degree (some students go on to do a 'top up' year to get a BA). They offer a work-based learning environment, where students will specialise in their chosen fashion subject and will often spend more time in the work-place than in the class-room. Opportunites are given to develop practical and technical skills with a relevant employer throughout the course, often leading to full-time offers of employment upon graduation.
HIGHER EDUCATION	DEGREE (most fashion courses will be BA, which is Bachelor of Arts)	3 or 4 YEARS (4 year courses include a year spent working in the industry on a work placement – these courses are called 'sandwich' courses)	This level of study is what most people (but not all) in the fashion industry focus towards, as these courses provide students with the opportunity to really specialise in a particular subject area. There are also general fashion courses, incorporating an overview of many areas of the industry (however most students specialise in one subject in their final year of study).

Most graduates enter employment from a BA course, while some extend their studies further via completion of an MA (Master of Arts), where they explore their specialist subject in further depth via extensive research and analysis. |

WHAT TYPE OF HOBBIES OR SKILLS COULD I PICK UP TO HELP PREPARE FOR A CAREER IN FASHION?

This depends on the sector of the industry you want to go into but, generally speaking, any other arts-based hobby will help to inspire you in your future fashion career/education. For instance, an involvement in amateur dramatics and the theatre will be of use if you decide to go into fashion show production, as you will gain an understanding of lighting, music and special effects. Photography skills will be useful later in your career if you go down the design or trend forecasting route, while language skills in French, Italian, Cantonese or Mandarin will be beneficial in nearly all fashion roles.

I'M TAKING A GAP YEAR – IS IT IMPORTANT THAT I USE THIS TIME TO GAIN EXPERIENCE OR WOULD WORK IN RETAIL FOR THE YEAR BE HELPFUL ENOUGH?

Unless you specifically want to work in retail management following university, I'd advise a mixture of working in retail and doing some work experience. It's never too early to begin getting relevant experience on your CV, and will be a huge advantage once you've graduated.

However, most work placements are unpaid, so it would be best to secure a part-time retail job to help fund your gap year (or enable you to save some money for university). Three days a week working in a store and the other two days doing a placement would be ideal. Also use this year to try a couple of different work experience placements in order to establish which sector of the industry interests you most. Then you'll be more prepared when it comes to specialising in a specific sector during your time at uni. *(See the final chapter of this book for more information on securing work experience.)*

I'D LIKE TO HAVE MY OWN FASHION BRAND ONE DAY – WHAT WOULD YOU ADVISE?

While it's great to have big ambitions, my advice is that you shouldn't jump into starting your own business too early in your career or without any fashion education or work experience. Very few people make it in the fashion world without having any prior exposure to the industry. Most of those who have launched their own successful labels without training or experience are likely to have already made quite a lot of money within another sector, enabling them to invest in a new business. Starting a new brand takes a huge amount of time, effort and cash – much more than most people realise – and there's enormous competition in the market place, with many other brands competing to survive. I'd always advise any aspiring independent designer to gain some official qualifications at university, where you'll not only learn essential technical skills, but also meet people on the course who will be useful contacts in years to come. This is where you will build up your future support network.

Once you've graduated, it's best to work in the industry within a major company for a couple of years before launching your own label – don't rush into it straight from uni. Working in the studio of an established company will again give you the opportunity to build important contacts (with factories, suppliers, buyers, production staff and other designers), who may all be useful to you later on. You will also gain a better understanding of what makes a commercial collection, what the pitfalls of the industry are and what is viable when it comes to production, saving you costly mistakes in the future. And, of course, working for a few years will give you the chance to build up some savings to invest in your future business – the more the better!

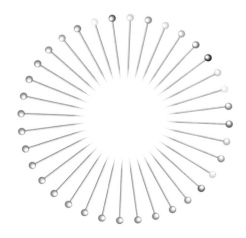

Image: Julie Bouiguerourene

Throughout this book you'll find an overview of qualifications required for each sector in the industry, and within each chapter I've included suggestions for a couple of specialist courses relating to the subject. Note that these are examples only, and in no way should you take these as being the only options available — they are intended as a brief introduction to what's on offer, and you are strongly encouraged to do your own comprehensive research to find out the most suitable options for you.

There are thousands of fashion courses to choose from at universities and colleges across the UK, Europe and further afield. It would take an entire book to list them all, so here are a couple of useful websites you can search on for courses at college and university, plus sites you can use to gain more information on general education topics.

UCAS
www.ucas.ac.uk
UCAS is the official organisation responsible for managing applications to higher education throughout the UK. Their site offers a wealth of advice for both students and parents, outlining courses on offer (extensive course finder and university listings), a section on student loans and grants, and important information on how to apply for university, how to manage the process, and useful dates/news.

HOT COURSES
www.hotcourses.com
Very comprehensive site that enables viewers to search for courses at sixth form, college and university level (undergraduate degrees and postgraduate degrees). There's also the option to narrow down the choices by location and study type (full-time, part-time or distance learning).

Not only can you find out about the courses available, there are also listings on each educational institution relating to information on fees and funding, location, accommodation on offer, student profiles and open days. For many courses, you can also read reviews from current students and graduates as to what they thought of their course and whether they would recommend it or not.

In addition, there is information regarding studying overseas and the different courses available.

ARTS THREAD
www.artsthread.com
While the two previous websites listed are general education sites, Arts Thread is a specialist creative arts site where you can gain more in-depth information on fashion/accessories/textiles courses. There is a course finder, plus interview tips and guidance on preparing a portfolio for entry to college/uni, written in collaboration with lecturers from well-known courses throughout the UK.

FOUNDATION DEGREE FORWARD
www.fdf.ac.uk
Course finder search site.

CHAPTER ONE: DESIGN

FRINGED + BEADING

IN THIS CHAPTER:

Illustration: Alice Jackman, c/o Topshop

WHAT DOES A FASHION/ACCESSORIES DESIGNER DO?

Many people think that being a designer involves simply drawing pictures all day. While that's a major part of the job, designers do much more than sketch. The process begins with deciding on a mood/theme for the collection and gathering inspiration by visiting exhibitions, people watching (on the street and at events such as music festivals), and researching trends online, at shows and via forecasting companies.

This research finishes with the designer producing a mood/theme board, including ideas for shape/silhouette, colour palette and fabric/materials. Gaining inspiration from these boards, they sketch lots of product ideas, which is called design development. As well as working on shape, designers are often expected to produce ideas for textiles/graphics. Following the development stage, the team then decides on the best designs to go to the sample stage. Designers create specification drawings to be sent to the factories, which include measurements for the garment/accessory, plus guidance on type of fabric, trims and fastenings to be used. The designer sources fabrics/trims and communicates with factories on the development of samples. Once the samples are finished, the designer meets with their buyers/sales agents to decide which pieces are successful enough to go into the stores.

Designers decide early in their career which category to focus on, choosing from outerwear, separates, jersey, tailoring, knitwear or evening/occasionwear. In addition, designers may specialise in womenswear, menswear or kidswear. There are also niche areas, including denim, bridalwear, surf/outdoor clothing, corporatewear (uniforms), lingerie, swim- and nightwear. Accessories designers choose from footwear, bags, belts, small leather goods, luggage, gloves, hats (millinery) or jewellery.

WHO EMPLOYS DESIGNERS?

Most designers work full-time, although many work on a freelance basis too. While most of the designers you hear about on TV and in magazines are those with their own label (like Matthew Williamson and Giles Deacon), these people make up only a small percentage of the fashion world, with the majority employed by a major company instead. Some will work with luxury brands (such as Gucci, Chanel and Burberry), either on couture (made-to-measure pieces) or on ready-to-wear – expensive collections that sell in stores across the world.

Many designers work for mid-market brands. These are cheaper than luxury brands but still have their own style (casual like Abercrombie & Fitch, edgy like Whistles, or sports brands like Nike and Adidas).

The majority of designers work for high-street retailers, such as Topshop and River Island. They work on 'fast fashion', so called because stores can turn around collections very quickly, from first seeing trends on the catwalks, to getting product into store. Designers may also work for suppliers and manufacturers (which design or produce ranges for other companies), or even for supermarket chains that have their own ranges (e.g. George at Asda).

KEY WORKING RELATIONSHIPS

Most designers work in a team, which generally includes production staff, pattern cutters, seamstresses, product developers, trend forecasters, and textile and graphic designers. One of the key relationships is with buyers, who decide which designs go into stores.

RELATED ROLES

Throughout their career, designers may cross over to roles in trend forecasting, illustration, product development and CAD design.

WORKING HOURS

Usually 8.30am–6pm, but many designers work much longer hours. At the luxury/couture end of the market, they're expected to work round the clock when it's show time. This job tends to be one where you don't switch off, as designers are always on the lookout for inspiration.

SALARY

This depends on location – salaries are usually higher at companies located in major cities. Assistants: £14–£19k. Junior or mid-level designers: £19–£35k. Senior designers: £32–£55k. Head designer/design director: £50–£120k or more.

EDUCATION:

Useful subjects to study at high school/sixth form: Art & Design, Textiles, Graphics, Fashion

Higher education: There are a huge number of courses — here are a few of the specialist options:
- Nottingham Trent University: BA (Hons) Fashion Knitwear Design
- Cordwainers (London): Foundation & BA degrees in footwear, accessories and lingerie
- De Montfort University: BA (Hons) Contour Fashion
- London College of Fashion: BA (Hons) Bespoke Tailoring
- Leeds College of Art: BTEC HNC Millinery

BEST THINGS ABOUT THE JOB

- Getting to travel and experience new cultures
- Seeing your designs in stores, and even better, people wearing them!
- Going shopping is classed as research!
- Having the opportunity to create beautiful things

WORST THINGS ABOUT THE JOB

- Sometimes not being able to switch off from thinking about design
- The hours can be long and erratic
- Being away from home for long periods when travelling

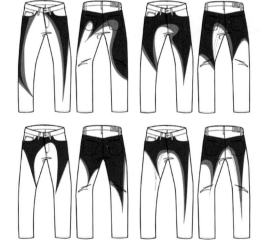

"If you want a 9-5 job, this is not the kind of career you should be pursuing"

Michele Palma, Design Director

WHAT SKILLS ARE NEEDED TO WORK IN DESIGN?

- A creative eye
- A flair for colour, texture and patterns
- Good drawing ability and CAD skills
- Excellent communication skills
- Ability to evaluate your own work and also accept constructive criticism
- Knowledge of the footwear and clothing market and future trends
- An understanding of different textile components and production
- The ability to manage a budget
- Excellent organisational skills
- To work well alone, as well as in a team environment

Illustrations: Left, Andy Thompson. Right: Mohsin Sajid, (C) LEVI'S JAPAN K.K / OKI-NI LTD

Alice has been the Womenswear Designer at Topshop since 2008. She has 10 years experience working on womenswear for the high street and has specialised in denim for six years. Here she shares what it's like to work for such a major fashion company.

Industry Insider!

EDUCATION:
School: Art, English, History, Maths, Sciences
A-levels: English, French, Classics
University: BA (Hons) degree in Fashion Marketing & Design at University of Northumbria

WHAT WAS YOUR CAREER PATH BEFORE TOPSHOP?

I began by doing two work placements while at uni — one at Debenhams and the other in India at a supplier. I learnt loads from both. My first job was with a small denim company based in London as a design assistant. I then worked for high-street brands and suppliers and also spent some time working freelance.

WHAT DO YOU THINK SET YOU APART FROM OTHER APPLICANTS WHEN YOU GOT YOUR JOB?

First impressions count so, first and foremost, it's important to be friendly and approachable. You should also believe in yourself and your ability and, lastly, you have to love the brand you want to work for. I tried to cover all of the above!

WHAT SORT OF PRODUCT DO YOU DESIGN?

Denim, including jeans, shorts, playsuits, jackets, shirts, etc.

WHAT DO YOU DO ON A DAILY BASIS?

I work closely with my buyer to make sure nothing is missing and we have all the key shapes, fabrics and washes for each seasonal trend. I also attend design meetings, create trend/fabric boards, do research and often do presentations. The role involves liaising with suppliers, briefing them on what we need — i.e. new styles, fabrics, trims. I also go to fabric mills to see the latest denim developments, and also to trim suppliers for buttons, rivets and branding. And of course the designing takes up a large part of the day.

WHAT'S THE FAVOURITE COLLECTION/STYLE YOU'VE WORKED ON?

At Topshop we have our own catwalk collection called 'Unique' that we show at London Fashion Week every season. This is definitely a perk of working for Topshop as we can be very creative and develop some amazing techniques, fabrics and styles. My favourite was the Spring/Summer 2010 show — the theme was based on surf culture and I designed some really destroyed, sun-bleached denim with badges and hand-stitching details.

IS IT EXCITING WHEN YOU SEE YOUR PRODUCT ON THE SHOPFLOOR, OR PEOPLE WEARING IT ON THE STREET?

It's always exciting seeing someone buy and wear the product. It's also great when you flick through magazines and see a fashion shoot using one of your pieces or someone famous wearing it.

HOW MANY DESIGNS DO YOU HAVE TO DO EACH SEASON, AND HOW MANY ARE ACTUALLY PUT INTO PRODUCTION?

It's hard to answer that, as we have to continually develop product to make sure we're on top of all the trends and first on a trend before anyone else, so it can sometimes seem like a lot. However, the buyer and merchandiser allocate the departmental spend each season, so as a team we have a rough idea of how many styles we need to do. We look at the previous season and how we can capitalise on the success of a key silhouette or a previous best-seller. We prioritise our core styles (e.g. a basic skinny jean) and make sure we have an update in the key washes. After that we work on fashion styles and if we have money left we can trial directional styles in small volume for the Oxford Circus store in London or the online store. The hit rate of sampling to shop floor is pretty good — I would say about 70 per cent makes it into store.

HOW DO YOU GO ABOUT CHOOSING WHICH STYLES GO INTO PRODUCTION?

I work with the buyer to build the range. Anything we think is key goes in, and we might hold back some styles for a later date or the following season in a different wash and fabric.

Alice looking intrigued

IS YOUR JOB EXCITING AND GLAMOROUS? It's very exciting. Glamorous probably isn't the right word to use, but it's creative, inspiring and, most of all, fun.

WHAT'S THE BEST THING ABOUT YOUR JOB? The people – Topshop is full of lovely people and it feels a bit like a family. We also get to travel a lot. I recently went to LA for shopping then flew to Palm Springs for the Coachella Festival, which was amazing and really inspirational – it was great to see what people were wearing and how they were styling themselves.

WHAT ARE THE PERKS OF WORKING FOR A WELL-KNOWN STORE? Getting discount is great and the sample sales are really good – my wardrobe has grown hugely since I started working there. Meeting interesting people and sometimes the odd celebrity is good fun too.

DO YOU CONSIDER SUSTAINABILITY AT TOPSHOP? Yes, we feel very strongly about sustainability and make sure we include Fairtrade denim and also recycled pieces, and we're looking to increase this. We're also sourcing organic cotton for the range for next season. The denim mills we use are eco-friendly and have sustainability processes in place such as water re-processing, where the water used to wash the denim is cleaned and put back into the environment without the chemicals from the denim-washing process. Our carbon footprint is kept in check when allocating fabric to suppliers by choosing those nearest to the fabric source.

- SHORTEN LENGTH @ INSEAM BY 2.5CM

- ADD POCKETS AS SEEN - POCKETS TO BE BELLOW AS JACKET SAMPLE

- ADD 2 X BACK POCKET FLAPS ON BACK YOKE

-RAISE BACK YOKE BY 2CM

- 2 X BUTTON FASTENING AT FRONT

2 X BUTTONS TO BE 17MM

ADD ANOTHER BACK POCKET LEFT HAND SIDE AS WORN.

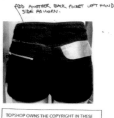

TOPSHOP OWNS THE COPYRIGHT IN THESE DESIGNS AND WILL TAKE ACTION IN THE EVENT OF THAT COPYRIGHT BEING INFRINGED

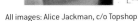

All images: Alice Jackman, c/o Topshop

Michele Palma is Design Director for the Versus collection at Gianni Versace in Milan, where he manages a team of designers across womenswear, menswear and accessories. He's worked for some of the most well-known companies in fashion — read on to find out how he got such an amazing career.

Industry Insider!

EDUCATION
- School subjects: Art & Design, Languages
- College: Foundation Studies in Art & Design at London College of Fashion
- University: BA degree in Fashion Design at Central St. Martin's College of Art & Design, London

HOW DID YOU GET TO WHERE YOU ARE NOW? I got my first job at John Galliano and Dior through Howard Tangye, Head of Womenswear at Central St Martin's. They contacted him to get names of new graduates and he sent me forward for an interview. I ended up working in Paris during the week and commuting back to London at weekends. After a few years, I'd had enough of travelling and, thanks to a well-known English headhunter, I moved back to London for a role with Burberry. I was then recommended to Calvin Klein and they offered me a job in New York. I got my last job at Versace by sending my CV directly to their HR Director. I've always been determined to succeed and that's how I got where I am now.

WHAT DO YOU THINK EMPLOYERS LIKE SO MUCH ABOUT YOUR WORK? I think what they love most is that I'm versatile and can work across all aspects of a collection, including wovens, knits, and accessories for both womenswear and menswear. I've always been able to understand the DNA of each fashion house that I've worked for and brought new ideas by interpreting the vision of each different Creative Director. I'm also capable of producing experimental designs as well as more wearable and commercial pieces, a balance that's very important when working for a well-known fashion house at a luxury level.

← Michele looking serious

DID YOU DO AN INTERNSHIP WHEN YOU WERE AT COLLEGE? I did a year at Hardy Amies on Savile Row in London. It used to be an English couture house, famous for being the dressmaker to HM Queen Elizabeth II. It was an extraordinary experience as I worked closely with some very talented dressmakers — I couldn't take my eyes off them while they were draping beautiful and expensive fabrics on the mannequins. I learnt how to sew by hand and how to tailor a garment correctly.

WHAT DOES AN AVERAGE DAY INVOLVE? I get to work early to make sure I have time on my own to organise the day ahead. Every day is different, according to each stage of the collections. At the beginning of each collection I spend entire days doing research with my team. We study books, buy/rent vintage clothes, and do research trips abroad. Sometimes I spend days choosing fabrics, and others doing clothes fittings. Two or three times a week I meet with the Creative Director to discuss the progress of each collection.

HOW MUCH CREATIVE FREEDOM DO YOU HAVE IN YOUR JOB? At the moment I have great freedom, especially at the start of each collection. It's important to work in close contact with the Creative Directors and exchange ideas to make sure we always produce something new and innovative. It's also essential to work closely with the marketing department, as they know what other fashion houses are doing in terms of products and also what our clients are asking for.

WHAT HAS BEEN THE MOST EXCITING MOMENT IN YOUR CAREER SO FAR? Every time I get a new job offer I get very excited. I also love working with well-known creative directors who have been able to turn around the company they represent by making them a very profitable brand. Living in different parts of the world has also been very exciting, getting to know

how French, English, American and Italian fashion houses really are.

HAVE YOU EVER THOUGHT ABOUT LAUNCHING YOUR OWN LABEL? Yes, but I worry about being out of a paid job and the security that comes with it. You often hear of young designers going bankrupt and struggling to get to the next stage in their business. You need a lot of money and people with good skills around you to make sure you have a successful business.

All images: Michele Palma

Mohsin is Senior Denim Designer for DKNY Jeans International, based in Singapore. He specialises in menswear, and throughout his career has worked with many well-known brands including OKI-NI, Firetrap, Edwin Europe, Alfred Dunhill, Pringle of Scotland, John Richmond and Puma.

Industry Insider!

EDUCATION
- School: Life Drawing, Pottery, Photography, Jewellery, Maths, English
- College: Northbrook College – National Diploma in Fashion & Textiles
- University: Westminster University – BA (Hons) Fashion Design

WHAT INSPIRED YOU TO BECOME A FASHION DESIGNER? When I was still at school, I used to collect all *The Sunday Times Style* magazines for one reason only: Julie Verhoeven. Her amazing illustrations were published every week, and I used to treasure them and study them. She alone is the reason I went into fashion.

WHAT DOES YOUR JOB ENTAIL? I design about 30–40 new types of jeans per season, which involves looking at new trends, whether new types of washes, or new fits. I keep a very close eye on what's new and interesting, not necessarily in fashion. The actual design part of the job is quite small. Most of the time I'm sending emails, confirming fabrics/trims, communicating with factories – updating specs if details have changed – and having meetings with directors to present new ideas.

IS IT HARD TO FIND A JOB AS A FASHION DESIGNER? Yes, but you should try to work for a brand you admire, work for free, get your foot in the door, and then make yourself indispensable. When I graduated I was one of a handful of designers who used Illustrator and Photoshop. OKI-NI was looking for an intern who had these skills to help out (no pay, just travel expenses), and I jumped at the chance. I ended up staying on, and left three years later as a Senior Designer. The thing is, I worked hard at college

and always pushed myself and that's what helped me get my first job. That I wasn't getting paid didn't bother me. I waited nine months before I got my first regular paycheck, but it was worth the sacrifice.

DID YOU DO AN INTERNSHIP WHEN YOU WERE STILL AT COLLEGE? Yes, with one of my heroes, Julian Roberts, who is one of the most creative pattern-cutting masters. I worked for him throughout my years at university, helping with pattern cutting, sewing and CAD work, and learned a lot that inspired me to do complicated pattern work, and really push myself as a young designer.

WHICH DESIGN OR COLLECTION HAVE YOU BEEN MOST PROUD OF? My work at OKI-NI, especially the collections for Levi's and Aquascutum. But I would say designing the entire Pringle of Scotland '1815' menswear range was one of my proudest achievements, including wovens, jersey knitwear and also graphics and branding. The best part was seeing it all in a showroom presented in the way I designed it and putting together looks for the fashion show.

HOW DO YOU COME UP WITH NEW DESIGNS? It starts with one strong idea or focus point – things are much easier if you have a theme – then I research like crazy. I then start thinking about fabrics, pocket shapes, trims, graphics – mini stories inside stories. It should naturally come together, if you have a strong idea.

HOW MANY DESIGNS ARE YOU EXPECTED TO DO FOR EACH COLLECTION, AND HOW MUCH TIME ARE YOU GIVEN TO CREATE EACH ONE? It's different at every company. At DKNY I do 30–40 pieces per season, and the design phase is a month long. At John Richmond I worked on 180 pieces per season.

Mohsin and the giant Coke!

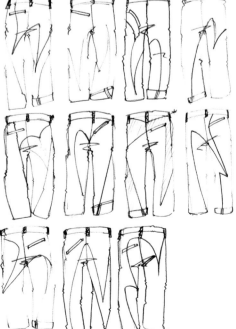

All images: Mohsin Sajid, (C) LEVI'S JAPAN K.K / OKI-NI LTD

Viki has 13 years of design experience and is Accessories Design Director at Lulu Guinness, London. She has an amazing CV, having worked for Calvin Klein, Club Monaco and Pringle. Viki designs handbags, small leather goods, umbrellas, luggage, eyewear, jewellery, bed linen, shoes and scarves.

Industry Insider!

EDUCATION
- School: Maths, English, French, Chemistry, Biology, History, RE, Art
- A-levels: Art, English, Communication/Media Studies, General Studies
- College: Foundation course in Art & Design
- University: BA (Hons) degree in Fashion Marketing at the University of Northumbria, Newcastle

DID YOU DO WORK EXPERIENCE AT COLLEGE? Yes, and I think it's really important to try out a few areas if you're not 100 per cent sure what you want to do. I was convinced I'd work in the business side of fashion, but found I preferred design.

HOW DID YOU GET YOUR FIRST JOB? A talent scout for Calvin Klein saw my portfolio at Graduate Fashion Week and asked if I'd like to be interviewed. After that I had to do a project, then was offered the job and joined their team in New York six months after graduation.

WHAT MADE YOU DO ACCESSORIES INSTEAD OF GARMENT DESIGN? Many things. First, it was a whirlwind moving to NY to work somewhere as prestigious as Calvin Klein, so I was in awe of everything and everyone there. I had amazing training, by very talented people, so accessories design became a passion very quickly. I love the attention to detail in accessories and adore finding beautiful leathers, working with artisans in Italy to create a special piece. One of the main things I love about bags is that they're not fitted to the body, so there are no restrictions in terms of fit. They're all-inclusive – whatever shape or size you are, a well chosen accessory can really lift your outfit. I also like that they're essentially practical things – you need a bag to put your things in, shoes to protect your feet, a belt to keep your trousers up.

IS WORKING AS AN ACCESSORIES DESIGNER AS YOU EXPECTED IT TO BE? Yes, but hard work. I'm always looking for ideas, on the journey to work, on holiday, all the time. I'm never without my sketchbook and camera.

WHAT TECHNIQUES DO YOU USE IN YOUR DESIGNS? I prefer hand sketching as I don't think you can replicate the idea/feel of something as well unless you illustrate it by hand. However, it's also useful to be able to use Photoshop/Illustrator to support your hand sketches.

WHERE DO YOU GET INSPIRATION? It can be from people I see on the street, vintage pieces, 'tear sheets' (newspaper/magazine cuttings), bits of old fabric I found in my parents' attic and, depending on which company I'm working for, the company archive.

ARE THERE BAG TRENDS OR DO YOU FOLLOW GENERAL FASHION TRENDS? It depends on the company. Some follow trends, others edit trends, some create trends. There's lots of interesting prediction info out there, but it depends on which level of the market you're working at as to whether it's relevant.

HOW LONG DOES IT TAKE TO DEVELOP A BAG COLLECTION? It varies. Normally, there are three to four seasons a year for which a separate collection needs to be designed, so you often have to work at a faster pace than you'd like. But the added pressure helps to focus the mind.

HOW MUCH TRAVEL DO YOU DO? Depending on the company, it could be monthly trips to Italy, or seasonal trips to the Far East to visit factories to get the bags looking exactly as you want. There are also annual trade shows – essential for sourcing new leathers/materials and meeting with tannery owners to develop a good working relationship with them.

Viki at her desk in the Lulu Guinness Studio, London →

Andy is Head of Men's Footwear Design for Lloyd Shoes Ltd, where he's responsible for the Burton and Ben Sherman accounts. Previous roles include design for River Island, Nicole Farhi, French Connection and Mizuno Sports. With 12 years of experience, Andy has worked on formal, casual and sports shoes.

Industry Insider!

EDUCATION:
- School: Maths, English, Science, Geography, RE, History, Art, CDT
- A-levels: Art, English, Economics
- University: BA degree in Product Design at Central St Martin's College of Art & Design, London

DID YOU DO WORK EXPERIENCE AT COLLEGE? Yes, I worked at Fila. This was invaluable as it gave me an insight into practices that are essential in a professional environment.

DID YOU GO INTO ACCESSORIES IMMEDIATELY AFTER GRADUATION? No, I had a few short-term contracts including CAD, working on clothing, accessories and footwear. Other jobs included trend analysis for a design and marketing company.

WHAT MADE YOU GET INTO FOOTWEAR? From a young age I've been fascinated with footwear, in particular sneakers, as they play a big role in today's popular culture. I'm also interested in the technical aspects of footwear design.

HOW DO YOU COME UP WITH NEW DESIGNS? I have a multi-faceted approach before starting to design — this way I feel the end result has a more individual slant. Research is part of the initial process, which stimulates my mind, opening up different avenues of interest, and helps me visualise shape, structure, colour and detail. Next is the initial sketching and I get two things from this: first, after the research stage, I need to get down all my ideas on paper; second, sketching helps me put ideas into a more definitive form. From this I can then put first prototypes into work.

WHAT TECHNIQUES DO YOU USE IN YOUR DESIGNS? I use sketches, material swatches, and CAD images in presenting my designs (created on programs such as Photoshop and Illustrator).

DO YOU GET TO TRAVEL IN YOUR JOB? I'm fortunate in being able to travel all over the world, including Tokyo, New York, Paris and Amsterdam. I go overseas two to three times per season and experience lots of different cultures and meet interesting people.

WHERE DO YOU GET THE INSPIRATION FOR YOUR WORK? From travel, and I always have my sketchbook to draw inspiration from. I also create a photo diary of trips — a valuable tool in understanding different environments and capturing detail.

WHICH SHOE DESIGNERS INSPIRE YOU? Tinker Hatfield from Nike — he's behind many design classics such as Air Jordans III through to Air Jordans XV. To most footwear designers, he is a shoe genius. Also, Hiroki Nakamura (VisVim) — every shoe design has a strong identity and meticulous attention to detail.

HOW LONG DOES IT TAKE TO DEVELOP A SHOE COLLECTION? Having had experience working on brands and also for retailers, I have found the time you have to develop ranges varies greatly. Working for a branded footwear company you usually have to work one to two years ahead on seasonal ranges. The ranges are smaller, which allows brands to push the boundaries on innovation. Working for retailers is different, as designers work closer to the season and the ranges are larger.

Andy looking surprised!

All images: Andy Thompson

We've put your questions to a team of industry insiders who all have extensive experience of working in fashion/accessories design. Our experts include Alice Jackman, Viki Wittering, Andy Thompson, Mohsin Sajid and Michele Palma – read more about their exciting careers on the previous pages. They are joined by Menswear Design & Development Manager for Liberty of London, James Watson, who has also worked for TopMan.

WHAT ARE YOUR TOP TIPS FOR ASPIRING DESIGNERS?

Always ask for feedback – it's the only way you learn and improve. Also, have a passion for product, be persistent and use every opportunity as experience.
ANDY THOMPSON

Along with your creative skills, I think it's really simple: work hard and be nice to people.
VIKI WITTERING

Enjoy what you do, be passionate about it and keep updated on the trends – catwalks, magazines, blogs and what people are wearing on the street.
ALICE JACKMAN

Start looking at designers, collections and brands that interest you, and try and figure out what you like about each designer. Read fashion magazines and start looking at blogs, and work out what gets you excited about design.
MOHSIN SAJID

IS IT HARD TO GET A JOB WITH A WELL-KNOWN BRAND?

You need to make sure that if you're going for a job at a well-known brand you research them well and understand what their 'look' is. Also establish how you can contribute to the brand and their success and if your style is suited to them. At Topshop, I began freelancing two days a week and was taken on permanently within two months of starting.
ALICE JACKMAN

IS A DEGREE REQUIRED TO WORK IN DESIGN?

Yes, most people have a degree. I think it gives you the grounding and experience that you need to work in the industry, and is definitely the norm these days.
VIKI WITTERING

I'M STILL AT HIGH SCHOOL – HOW CAN I GO ABOUT GETTING WORK EXPERIENCE IN DESIGN?

Make a definitive list of organisations you would love to work for. Think very carefully about what you'd like to achieve from your prospective placement. From this, write speculative letters and call companies/individuals.
ANDY THOMPSON

IS IT HARD TO FIND A JOB AS A DESIGNER?

Yes, you have to really want it to make it work. It's not an easy career path and it takes a lot of effort, but if you work hard and effectively it can be very rewarding.
JAMES WATSON

WHAT SHOULD A WANNABE DESIGNER HAVE IN THEIR PORTFOLIO?

Strong sketch work. This highlights many things including your thought process, idea generation and ability to communicate 2D into a 3D form.
ANDY THOMPSON

DO YOU HAVE TO BE GOOD AT DRAWING TO BE A DESIGNER?

I don't think it's just about being good at drawing, it's also about being a great communicator. You can communicate in many different ways, e.g. mood boards, brainstorming, montages, observations.
ANDY THOMPSON

No, a good designer knows how to make the overall look work, and this doesn't necessarily involve traditional art skills. It's more important to know how to create the feel of the collection so that it's appropriate for the target market.
JAMES WATSON

It definitely helps. You have to be able to get your ideas across to lots of people, and usually drawing is the easiest way to do this. I sometimes work three dimensionally, to get across the shape and proportion of a piece. For instance, I sometimes make a paper or card model, or sew pieces together on the sewing machine if it's a softer, less structured shape I'm trying to achieve.
VIKI WITTERING

Image: Michele Palma

DO YOU THINK THAT HAVING GOOD EXAM GRADES MATTERS IF I WANT TO GO INTO FASHION DESIGN?

It can only be a good thing if your grades are good — and being multi-skilled is always a bonus, especially in key languages such as Italian. It really helps if you're able to speak a second language.
JAMES WATSON

DO YOU THINK IT'S ESSENTIAL TO LIVE IN A BIG CITY TO FIND WORK AS A DESIGNER?

Not always, but it really does help to have a network of colleagues/friends in the industry, and this is made easier by spending time in fashion capitals.
JAMES WATSON

I chose a big city, mainly because of all the art galleries and shops and because it's harder to get inspiration and people watch if you're not near the action.
MOHSIN SAJID

AS A DESIGNER, DO YOU GET TIME FOR A SOCIAL LIFE?

The more responsibilities you have at work, the less of a social life you end up having, but I guess that's true of any job. You just need to find the right balance between your job and what you actually need as a person. I have a great relationship with my team and we often get together after work or during the weekend. You can end up working weekends and very long hours in this business but then you also get some periods where it's less hectic and you can go to work later in the morning and leave earlier in the day. I can definitely tell you that if you're looking for a 9–5 job then this is certainly not the kind of career that you should be pursuing.
MICHELE PALMA

HOW DO YOU COME UP WITH NEW IDEAS SEASON AFTER SEASON?

I spend time with the Creative Director to find out what direction to take for the collection. We discuss themes, colours, fabrics and silhouettes. I then start doing research with my team making sure that we aren't working on something that other fashion houses have already done. It's very helpful when you are designing to have a look at what other designers are doing so that you can create something new. Although we often change direction throughout the designing process, we tend to stick to our initial ideas and carry them through until the end and believe in them. If you really believe in one idea,

it's easier to convince the customers to buy your product and it becomes less confusing for the press when they see the collection on the runway.
MICHELE PALMA

WHAT DOES NO ONE TELL YOU BEFORE YOU START OUT?

Your reputation is crucial so make sure it's impeccable. If you always work hard and over deliver, it's amazing how the right people get to know. Keep this in mind from the outset — it's a huge plus.
JAMES WATSON

Fashion is hard work. There's no other industry where every season you need to come up with something new every time, and lots of designers burn out.
MOHSIN SAJID

ARE THERE ANY PERKS TO WORKING IN FASHION/ACCESSORIES DESIGN?

Travel, as you get to see the world and meet incredible manufacturers. Also, the shopping trips are fun. (But you usually end up buying yourself clothes — it's kind of an occupational hazard. How you present yourself is important when you work in fashion so I'm always on the lookout for something interesting to add to my wardrobe.)
JAMES WATSON

You get to go to fashion shows and events. Also, you can dress how you like, as long as you're confident and believe in yourself and your own personal style. And if you're lucky you get given some samples along the way.
MOHSIN SAJID

Image: Michele Palma

To Do List

▶ **VIEW** as many fashion websites as you can — there are a huge number to choose from. Build up your knowledge of ones to get visually inspired by, sites for fashion business news (it's important to keep up to date with industry happenings), and sites you can look at to view the work of other designers (catwalk images as well as drawn work). Good ones include: **www.style.com / www.drapersonline.com / www.coroflot.com / www.londonfashionweek.co.uk / www.thecoolhunter.net**

"This site is really interesting to look at to get inspired by how people put outfits together": **www.thesartorialist.blogspot.com**
JAMES WATSON

▶ **PRACTISE** how to get your design ideas down on paper. As our experts have explained, you don't have to be the best drawer, but it definitely helps if you can produce work that looks realistic. Experiment with different materials for lots of different effects — charcoal, pencils, fine-liners, paints, marker pens (look out for flat markers such as Pantone pens — they cost more than normal felt tips, but produce great results). You will need to show evidence of your fashion ideas in a portfolio, whether for entrance to fashion college or for when you have work experience interviews, so it's important to build up as many projects as you can.

▶ **GET INSPIRED!** about different fabrics and materials. Research the properties of each one, find out what different fabrics are used for, and learn the names of them. This will stand you in good stead when it comes to putting a collection together at college/uni, or when you begin work experience. The more you know, the easier it will be. Visit fabric stores in your area — most towns and cities will have a few independent shops, and you should also find fabric sections in most major department stores and at markets. Have a look in the bargain bins for scraps of cheap fabric to buy to add to your projects, and also look out for interesting buttons, trims and fastenings. You don't have to spend a fortune — part of the fun is hunting for bargains. Begin to build up your collection of materials now, and you'll find it easier to get inspired in the future.

FTM
Fashion
and Textile
Museum

**FASHION &
TEXTILE MUSEUM**

**COURSES FOR
DESIGNERS**

AND THEY'RE
ONLY £120

* **Photoshop for Designers**
* **Illustrator for Designers**
* **InDesign for Designers**
* **Repeat Pattern using Photoshop**
* **Repeat Pattern using Illustrator**
* **Fashion Portfolio using Photoshop**
* **Lectra Kaledo Style**

Courses@FTM is offering 15 hour,
introduction, intermediate and
advanced level courses during the
day, at evenings and at weekends.
All courses are at our cutting edge
training centre near London Bridge.

To find out more call **020 7407 8664**
or email **info@ftmlondon.org**
www.ftmlondon.org/courses

83 Bermondsey Street, London SE1 3XF
⊖ ⇌ London Bridge

VISIT **WWW.FTMLONDON.ORG**
TO FIND OUT MORE ABOUT
OUR EXHIBITIONS,
WORKSHOPS AND
EVENTS

CHAPTER TWO: GRAPHICS & TEXTILES

IN THIS CHAPTER:

> "Being paid to doodle, sketch, draw and make pretty pictures all day is nice."

Matt Bibby, Fashion Graphic Designer

Images (from top): Sholto Drumlanrig / Matt Bibby / Sholto Drumlanrig

WHAT DOES A GRAPHIC/TEXTILE DESIGNER DO?

Working as a graphic or textile designer involves creating a distinctive visual identity for a company. In fashion this covers the design of pictures, patterns, surface decoration and lettering to be used on clothing, accessories, swing tickets, trims, labelling, posters, catalogues and websites.

This is a very competitive area of the industry, often with more graduates than jobs. Designers must therefore be very flexible and should be able to apply their ideas to lots of different companies and clients. Textile designers might specialise in one or two areas, which can include print, weave or knitted textiles or embroidery/embellishment. Graphic designers work on clothing, logo design, trims, labelling and swing tickets. In both professions, designers should ideally have an understanding of how to design for ladieswear, menswear, accessories, lingerie, sportswear and kidswear.

Working to a client brief, designers present their ideas in 2D or 3D format either as hand-drawn or painted designs, or more commonly using computer software such as Photoshop, Illustrator, InDesign, U4ia and Kaledo. This type of work is known as CAD (computer-aided design) and it allows the designer to produce realistic designs in lots of different colour-ways and formats in a short space of time.

WHAT TYPE OF COMPANY EMPLOYS TEXTILE AND GRAPHIC DESIGNERS?

Designers may work with brands, retailers, clothing suppliers, fabric manufacturers and graphic/textile design studios. Although all fashion companies use textile/graphic elements to a certain extent, it is brands (often casual, sports and streetwear brands) that use these elements most, in order to create a unique and distinctive style for their products. While some designers work full-time in house, the majority work on a freelance basis and are self-employed.

KEY WORKING RELATIONSHIPS

Textile and graphic designers will usually report to the Head of Design (in large organisations there may be a Head of Graphics and Head of Textiles), Design Director or Creative Director. They will also liaise with fashion and accessory designers, sales agents, buyers, art directors, copy editors and photographers.

RELATED JOBS

It is quite common for someone skilled in fashion textiles or graphics to work within other sectors alongside their usual fashion work, such as design for interiors (wallpaper, cushions, bed linen, rugs, towels and so on), gifts, stationery, small accessories, gift wrap and greetings cards. The elements used within textile design – such as use of colour and creation of inspiration boards – translate well into trend and colour forecasting work, and designers trained in textiles may cross over into this area. Print and graphic designers may also work solely in CAD roles which involves using software to create a realistic 2D or 3D representation of fabric, patterns or images.

WORKING HOURS

Most designers who are full-time for a company will work Monday–Friday between approximately 9am and 6pm. However, as with most roles in fashion, designers are often expected to work longer hours in order to meet deadlines. Freelancers will often work longer and more erratic hours in order to balance jobs for lots of different clients, market their work, find new jobs and chase clients for payment.

SALARY

Starting salary for a new graduate can range from £14k–£18k in a full-time role (or between £80 and £150 a day freelance). This varies considerably depending on location and type of organisation worked for. With a few years of experience a designer can expect approx £22k–£35k. Full-time senior or head designers can earn more than £40k per year, and freelancers between £200 and £400 per day.

Textile designers can earn extra income through selling designs/swatches of their work to textile agents, who pay them either a one-off amount for the piece or, more commonly, commission once they have sold the design to a client (the designer can typically receive 40–55 per cent commission).

EDUCATION: WHAT DO I NEED TO STUDY TO BECOME A GRAPHIC/TEXTILE DESIGNER?

Useful school/sixth form subjects: Art & Design, IT, Graphics, Fashion & Textiles, Media Studies

Here are a few suitable higher education courses:
- UCA, Farnham: Textiles for Fashion & Interiors (BA Degree)
- University of Brighton: Textile Design for Fashion with Business Studies (BA Degree)
- Newcastle College: Textile & Surface Design (Foundation Degree)
- Swansea Metropolitan University: Surface Pattern, Textiles for Fashion (BA Degree)
- University of East London: Fashion Futures with Graphic Design (BA Degree)
- Northumbria University: Fashion Marketing (BA Degree)
- Southampton Solent University: Fashion Graphics (BA Degree)

BEST THINGS ABOUT THE JOB

- Being paid to doodle, sketch, draw and essentially make pretty pictures and patterns all day, which is nice

- It's very creative and stimulating and you get to work with many different companies and people

WORST THINGS ABOUT THE JOB

- At its worst, you sit on your behind at a computer for hours trying to meet deadlines. I would say that being freelance can be tough. It's harder than you might think to sit on your own all day and stay motivated and focused. On the other hand, you can find yourself missing that peace and solitude when you work in a busy, loud and stressful office

- Being freelance can be hard work and sometimes the hours are quite extreme

Image: Matt Bibby

WHAT SKILLS ARE NEEDED TO BE A GRAPHIC/TEXTILE DESIGNER?
- Excellent visual communication skills — drawing, sketching, conveying ideas on paper
- Good computer skills — awareness of relevant programs and how to use them
- Graphic designers should have an understanding of typography (use of different fonts and layouts)
- Being a good listener and team player — you're designing graphics for another designer most of the time
- Good time management
- Ability to work to deadlines, be organised and self-motivated

Matt Bibby is a UK-based Fashion Graphic Designer. He's been working in the industry for nine years, starting out with TopMan on a freelance basis, then going on to work with brands such as Fenchurch, Gul, Russell Athletic, Wrangler and Fly53. Matt has worked as a full-time designer for Timberland, and is currently with Chunk Clothing. Here he gives the lowdown on what it's like to work in fashion graphics.

Industry Insider!

EDUCATION
- GCSEs: English Literature & Language, Maths, Science, Geography, Art, Design & Technology
- A-levels: Media Studies, Art & Design, Design & Communication
- College: BTEC Foundation Studies in Fashion Design at Cleveland Art College
- Degree: BA (Hons) Fashion Studies at the University of Derby

WHAT TYPE OF WORK DO YOU DO? As a graphic designer for clothing, I do everything from trend research, designing print and pattern, logo development, branding and trim design.

WHAT MADE YOU GET INTO GRAPHICS AND NOT GARMENT DESIGN? The appeal of the Fashion Studies BA at Derby was that it was a very flexible course and supported a wide spectrum of subjects so there was real encouragement to pursue any path you wanted. It was a sandwich course so I had to do a year's work experience which I did in Sydney, Australia, working for the local surf/skate brands as a graphic designer. I think I fell into that role through a general interest in graphics and print although I still loved designing garments. My final collection was a mix of both garment and print, but my portfolio was strongest on the graphics side of things so I attracted work in that area first.

WHAT DOES A FASHION GRAPHIC DESIGNER ACTUALLY DO? It varies. As a freelance graphic designer it's pretty simple. You get a brief and generally discuss it with the client. Then it's simply a case of developing the required number of prints. I use computer software like Adobe Illustrator the most but it depends on what the client wants. If they want sketchy, hand-drawn artwork then I'll sit with my art-box and draw/paint away before using the computer. When you're finished it's just a case of emailing the artwork or popping a CD in the post to the client.

If you've missed the target then you may have to re-work things, but that's avoidable by having a good brief and chat at the start of the project. In a full-time role or working in-house your role can vary greatly. In-house roles gave me experience designing labels and trims, buttons, branding, logos, look-books and catalogues, and analysing trends alongside designing graphics for garments.

WHAT TECHNIQUES DO YOU USE IN YOUR DESIGNS? I tend to doodle or sketch my designs first but I can do entire projects straight on the computer. I might sketch to see how the idea might fit together, but doodling is also a great way to create ideas or brainstorm around them. Once I'm happy with an idea in my mind's eye I have to get it into the computer. I begin by scanning sketches and reference material, then drawing with the software, using type and then colour.

HOW DO YOU GO ABOUT FINDING NEW JOBS?

Drumming up new clients takes a little nerve but can be quite easy. Magazines are a great place to start. I check out who's advertising, I check their website and see if I feel their product range has my kind of graphic work in there. If it looks like something I could do or even improve on I find the best thing is to call them directly and speak to the head of the design team. It can make you nervous and, if no one has work to offer, you can feel pressure to get earning some money. If you stay on top of your portfolio, keeping it updated regularly, then you're ready to knock on another door when one closes.

The alternative to doing it yourself is to find work via an agency. Recruitment agencies can be great at finding the work for you. Because they are both hired by the client and they know your work they can match you up with some great jobs.

WHERE DO YOU GET THE INSPIRATION FOR YOUR WORK?

You can never have enough design books on your shelf in my opinion. It is kinda goofy but the internet, while being a distraction at times, is also perfect for looking at trends, topics and finding that little gem that sparks a series of ideas. There are so many great design sites with news and features that I could spend (and probably have) an entire day browsing the web.

HOW MUCH DID YOU GET PAID WHEN YOU STARTED OUT AS A NEW GRADUATE?

I was earning £150 per day when I started freelance. It's gone up now, but you have to stay within what a client expects. You can juggle it a little, negotiate and discuss, but it's important not to sell your skills too cheaply.

HOW MUCH TRAVEL DO YOU DO IN YOUR JOB?

I've travelled a fair bit through permanent roles; inspiration trips, factory visits and trade shows have taken me across America, Europe and into Africa. As a freelancer I've travelled around the UK and Europe to work in-house with clients in their offices.

WHAT HAS BEEN YOUR FAVOURITE JOB/CLIENT AND WHY?

The best jobs are the ones that really match your tastes. I love working with FLY53 because the graphics are always edgy, a bit rock'n'roll, and the projects are so varied.

All images: Matt Bibby

Sholto is based in London and has 20 years of industry experience. He specialises in designing printed textiles for a wide range of clients including COS (owned by H&M), Fat Face, Liberty of London, Diane von Furstenberg and the V&A. Here he explains what a textile designer actually does and what's involved in the design process.

EDUCATION
- Degree: BA in Surface Pattern at Staffordshire University

DID YOU GO INTO TEXTILES IMMEDIATELY AFTER GRADUATION? IF NOT, WHAT DID YOU DO? After leaving Staffordshire University I secured a job within the design studio at Liberty.

WHAT MADE YOU GET INTO TEXTILES AND NOT GARMENT DESIGN?
I got on to my degree at Staffordshire to do graphic design but the course was structured so you had to try two other subjects before getting started. One of my choices was textile design and it was like a light going on. I absolutely loved it and changed from graphics to textile design.

IS WORKING AS A TEXTILE DESIGNER AS YOU EXPECTED IT TO BE?
Being a textile designer in many ways is exactly what I thought it would be and I find it very stimulating and creative. What I didn't realise when I left college was how competitive it can be.

WHAT DOES A TEXTILE DESIGNER ACTUALLY DO? IS IT SIMPLY DRAWING PICTURES AND IDEAS? A textile designer has to be able to interpret a brief that a company, manufacturer or designer gives them and create designs that fit their brand. In order to do this you need to be able to draw and paint well and, increasingly, have good computer skills. You also need to be able to colour designs into different looks and also put designs into repeat.

DO YOU HAVE TO BE A GOOD DRAWER TO BE A TEXTILE DESIGNER?
I think it is very important to be able to draw well as this is the essence of being a textile designer. Also you have to understand visual references and historical contexts, because fashion is very reference based.

WHAT WAS YOUR FAVOURITE WAY OF DESIGNING AND DEVELOPING PRINTS DURING YOUR EDUCATION AND WHICH METHODS DO YOU USE TODAY? I used to develop everything by hand but now find using computer programs for design makes the whole process much quicker and means I can develop many more ideas and do a lot more work in less time. That said, I think people can become far too reliant on design programs and it can give work an impersonal look. So it is important to keep that hand-drawn element and to sketch your ideas first.

WHAT TECHNIQUES DO YOU USE IN YOUR DESIGNS? I tend to draw or paint my work and use any number of techniques to do this. I then scan and manipulate work on the computer.

WHERE DO YOU GET THE INSPIRATION FOR YOUR WORK? Inspiration can come from any number of places. I go to exhibitions, look at magazines, shops and movies. You could literally get inspired to do a print looking at a piece of graffiti. It's everywhere!

WHAT HAS BEEN YOUR FAVOURITE JOB/CLIENT AND WHY? I love working for Liberty of London Print. I got my first job working in their design studio and I have continued to work in a freelance capacity for them over the years. I love the work they do, and the people who work there are really talented.

DID YOU HAVE TO WORK FOR FREE WHEN YOU STARTED OUT? I did do some work placements for free. I think it's good in terms of getting to know people and also having some hands-on experience. Also if you are interested enough in the work the company does this can show a level of commitment, and may lead to paid work further down the line.

HOW LONG DOES IT TAKE TO BEGIN TO GET PAID WORK? These days it's tough, and a combination of skill and luck is involved in how long it takes. Try and contact as many companies as you can and keep plugging away.

"Being a textile designer is exactly what I expected – very stimulating and creative."

Sholto Drumlanrig

All images: Sholto Drumlanrig

ASK THE EXPERT

We've put your questions on how to get into textiles/graphics to Matt Bibby and Sholto Drumlanrig, who are interviewed on the previous pages. They are joined by Luca Johnson, Senior Print Designer at River Island in London. She graduated in 2003 from Northumbria University, and landed her first job at Boxfresh. Luca's also worked on a freelance basis for Miss Selfridge, Topshop, Laura Ashley, TK Maxx and Next.

WHAT DOES AN AVERAGE DAY INVOLVE?

I spend a couple of hours a day researching and kicking ideas around while flicking through magazines and trawling the internet for trends and inspiration. I have about five sketchbooks on the go at once so one is always near when ideas pop up. Depending on the complexity of the designs I could spend the rest of the day working up between two and six ideas to a finished state. But I will also have meetings, developments and samples to check over, emergency rush jobs and all the other bits and bobs that come along to keep you on your toes.
MATT BIBBY

Most days I'm designing but I often have to go to client meetings to pick up a brief or present my work. I'm also keen to get out and about for inspiration – this could be looking at anything from an exhibition to a retailer.
SHOLTO DRUMLANRIG

WHAT ADVICE WOULD YOU GIVE TO SOMEONE WHO IS STILL AT SCHOOL ?

Start sketching as much as you can; being able to draw can only help and it doesn't hurt to improve your skills. If you can get some time playing with the software, like Adobe Photoshop and Illustrator, then that's great; you'll be banging out ideas in no time.
MATT BIBBY

Try to learn the basics of Photoshop/Illustrator – although books are perhaps hard to understand and learn from, ask around and see if anyone can show you the basics, then practise, practise, practise. Also contact businesses and ask if they do work experience at school level – my employer has students in over the summer holidays for one- or two-week placements.
LUCA JOHNSON

Have fun and be as creative as you can. There are no rules and you should explore and design things that you think are exciting. Your enthusiasm and enjoyment should show.
SHOLTO DRUMLANRIG

DO PEOPLE HAVE TO HAVE A DEGREE TO WORK IN FASHION GRAPHIC/TEXTILE DESIGN?

I'd say yes, based on the people I know in the industry but I don't think it's black and white. I look for a strong portfolio and good work experience; whether someone has a degree doesn't affect my decision a great deal.
MATT BIBBY

Most of the people I know who work in textile design have done a degree. I think it really helps because it gives you the time to learn skills and be creative. That said, you can do it yourself without a degree, but I think it is a harder road to travel.
SHOLTO DRUMLANRIG

HOW DO PEOPLE GET WORK EXPERIENCE IN FASHION GRAPHICS/TEXTILES?

Be confident and contact businesses — most have positions available for work experience. If you do get a placement, do the work asked of you but also offer to stay behind after working hours where you may be given the opportunity to do actual design work instead of photocopying! Nothing is more impressive than people working hard and going beyond what is asked. Believe me, you will get noticed if you exceed people's expectations!
LUCA JOHNSON

For work experience you'll need to be familiar with the relevant computer software, even if it's the very basics. If you can show an understanding of it during work experience interviews, it will get you far. Also, be enthusiastic at the interview stage and keen to learn once you actually get the job!
MATT BIBBY

DO MOST GRAPHIC/TEXTILE DESIGNERS WORK FREELANCE OR FULL-TIME?

I think most brands and clothing labels prefer a graphic designer in a full-time role, but there's a big market for freelancers to tap into. I've seen a lot of freelance roles develop into full-time jobs and vice-versa.
MATT BIBBY

WHAT ARE YOUR TOP TIPS FOR THOSE LOOKING TO GET INTO GRAPHICS/TEXTILES?

Get your portfolio looking as good as you can — it's all about visual communication. Because you're working on graphics for apparel it's very good to know about screen-printing and how graphics are applied. If you can build that knowledge, develop a portfolio of work and get some good experience you'll be well on your way.
MATT BIBBY

Know what you like and don't like and the reasons why. Understand how designers and retailers use print and how that changes from season to season. Read magazines and books. Draw and paint, find the best ways to create things and understand visually how print is created. And of course look at courses and higher education that offer training in the specifics of what interests you.
SHOLTO DRUMLANRIG

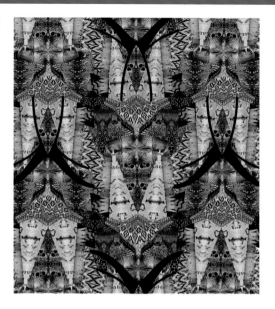

WHAT SHOULD A WANNABE GRAPHIC/TEXTILE DESIGNER HAVE IN THEIR PORTFOLIO?

You should show that you're able to take a project from brief through to final designs. If you can demonstrate your thought process then that's great. I like to see a variety of projects featuring different graphic styles, so they show flexibility. If a designer can show good idea development and sketches and their artwork is good, I'm always impressed. Oh, and keep the presentation simple; let the ideas and the artwork do the talking.
MATT BIBBY

I think someone wanting to be a textile designer should demonstrate creativity and a sense of diversity and show the process of a project, from the original brief through to the end print/design.
SHOLTO DRUMLANRIG

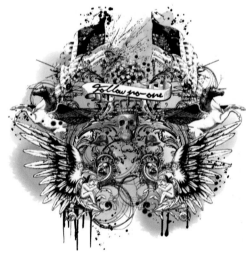

TELL US A SECRET ABOUT WORKING IN TEXTILES

That you can't be precious about the work you're producing — unlike at university/college where you have weeks to research an idea, you may only have an afternoon to research, sketch and produce the final print. Also, at least a basic knowledge of garment construction helps when considering the placement of prints. For instance, an understanding that certain techniques will not work over the seams of the garment is essential.
LUCA JOHNSON

WHAT ARE THE BEST WEBSITES TO LOOK AT FOR INSPIRATION?

Here are just a few:
www.patternity.co.uk
www.lobsterandswan.blogspot.com
www.stylebubble.typepad.com
www.ohjoy.blogs.com
www.ebay.co.uk
www.designspongeonline.com/category/sneak-peeks
LUCA JOHNSON

All images: Luca Johnson, c/o River Island

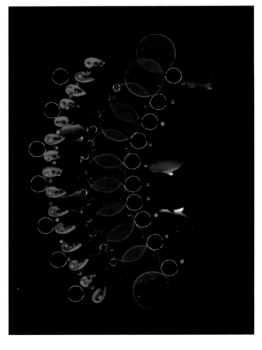

All images: Luca Johnson, c/o River Island

To Do List

▶ **RESEARCH** the work of other designers via online portfolio sites – this will give you a better idea of the standard of work you should ultimately aim towards. Remember that most of the designers presenting their images online will already have been in the industry for a few years, so don't be scared by the quality of the work if your own looks nothing like it! Take note of how designers present their mood boards, final designs and design development. Note what you think is interesting and why. Good sites to look at include:
www.coroflot.com / **www.styleapple.com** / **www.carbonmade.com**

▶ **DEVELOP** your computer skills. Even if you aren't in higher or further education at university or college yet, investigate options to do a short course, summer school or one-day workshop to study a relevant computer program. Having these skills will increase your chances of finding work experience, and will also impress tutors if you're looking to get on to a full-time college or uni course. Most towns and cities will have a college or training centre providing these types of courses. If you can't afford or can't find a course near you, perhaps club together with a friend who shares a similar interest in this to buy a book on the subject.

▶ **PRACTISE** your drawing skills constantly! As the designers featured in this chapter have mentioned, your drawn work is key to your success in this sector. It's no good having great design ideas if you can't execute them on paper, so get sketching, painting, doodling – buy a load of sketchbooks and fill them up!

▶ **GET INSPIRED!** It's very hard to come up with great design ideas unless you have lots of visuals to inspire you. Get out and about to view exhibitions at museums and galleries, and look at the graphics on products in lots of different stores, and at magazines for research on layout, fonts and graphic trends. People watch to see how others style themselves (it can be great to get ideas by seeing how they've put colours together or how they've used contrasting prints or textures in their outfit).

▶ **VISIT** the graduate design shows at your local college or university to see the work of up-coming designers at first hand. Most shows are in June/July. If you're based in or near London, it's worth going to the annual Graduate Fashion Week (**www.gfw.org.uk**) in early June. This is a visual showcase of work from fashion, textiles and accessories students who have graduated from courses across the UK and Europe. New Designers (**www.newdesigners.com**) in London is a similar event, with the focus more on textiles. This annual show takes place in June/July.

IN THIS CHAPTER:

beauty trends 2011:eyes & brows:year 2011:**turquoise brows**

Colored with a Crayola pencil is an image that comes to mind with these playfully naive and individual pale turquoise brows. An off-beat and playful expression is welcomed as these bleached-out brows get a tint of near-fluorescent color. Teamed with a nude face, these eyebrows make a fresh reference to minimal futurism. Alternatively complimentary orange eye-shadow continues a notion of optimism and makes fluorescent pastels a directional and brave choice.

start of report

next page >

Manish Arora Fall Winter 2010-11

Louise Gray Fall Winter 2010-11

Balenciaga Fall Winter 2010-11

WHAT DOES A TREND FORECASTER DO?

Have you ever wondered who decides when colours become fashionable, what makes us all wear similar styles, or why high-street shops all seem to have the same type of product at the same time? This is influenced by people called trend forecasters, who predict trends up to two years in advance, including a combination of different themes, colours, fabrics, shape and silhouette, graphics, patterns and textures. Forecasters usually work across a range of sectors, including womenswear, menswear and kidswear, while a few might specialise in areas such as lingerie or sportswear.

Most of their work is research-based, and they will use a number of different factors as the basis for what we will be wearing in a few years. This research doesn't focus only on fashion, but also social, cultural and economic influences. Forecasters use influences from art, music, film, books, theatre and consumer research (market research and visual information, e.g. photos of people who have an interesting 'look'), and then collate their findings as a series of key themes or trends.

They present this information to clients via trend boards, verbal and visual presentations, magazines, written trend reports and, increasingly through online presentations, websites, blogs and phone applications. Their clients include any company looking for information on what will be 'on trend' in the future, such as retailers, brands, ad agencies and design studios. Most trend agencies also work on other sectors apart from fashion, such as trends for the beauty industry, product design or interiors.

WHO EMPLOYS TREND FORECASTERS?

There are opportunities to work either full-time or freelance in this sector, but it is a small area of the industry, with more people wanting to get into it than there are jobs. Most people work for trend/colour forecasting agencies, usually located in major cities such as London, Paris and New York. Examples of trend agencies include Trendstop.com, Stylesignal, International Colour Authority, WGSN and Trend Union. A limited number of trend roles exist within brands, retailers and design consultancies.

KEY WORKING RELATIONSHIPS

Jaana Jätyri, CEO of Trendstop.com explains who else works within a trend agency: "At Trendstop.com we have researchers at junior, associate and senior levels, contributing trend-spotters, full-time and freelance street-style photographers, in-house picture researchers, trend, photo and sub-editors, photo re-touchers, publishers, fashion journalists, CAD, print, web and graphic designers, plus customer service staff, sales teams and international agents and resellers."

RELATED ROLES

Most trend forecasters have experience in other areas of the industry, and have worked either as fashion, accessories or textiles designers or within fashion marketing or journalism.

WORKING HOURS

Full-time employees work between approximately 9am–6pm, but it's very difficult to define when work starts and ends, because they're always looking out for interesting things, even outside normal working hours. Freelancers have to work whenever a project arises, so never have fixed hours.

SALARY

It can take a while to achieve a paid role, due to the sheer number of other people wanting the same job. Jaana Jätyri explains: "Entry-level positions receive lots of applications, which means that your first role is likely to be unpaid. However, this gets your foot in the door and a chance to prove yourself. If you are given this opportunity, do your utmost to demonstrate your skills. The initial salary might range £15k–£18k per year; a senior trend forecaster might earn £30k–£35k, while a trend manager would earn around £40k or more."

EDUCATION:

Useful school subjects: Art, Photography, English, Textiles, Languages, IT

Further education: There aren't many specialist courses in trend forecasting — most people come from courses in another sector, such as design, marketing, promotion or journalism. Here are a few of the specialist trend options:
- University of East London: BA (Hons) Fashion Futures — Trend Forecasting
- Polimoda (Florence, Italy): one-month Fashion Trends summer school course
- ESMOD University (Dubai campus): six-month Fashion Workshop — Trend Forecasting

BEST THINGS ABOUT THE JOB

We get to travel and visit the coolest music festivals — I'm off to Glastonbury next month to do a street style overview report, and can't think of anything better than chilling out watching some of my fave bands and photographing the cool trends on show.
RACHEL BANHAM, SENIOR TREND RESEARCHER AT TRENDSTOP.COM

Chosen for its fancied appropriateness to local tradition, we borrow from celebration dressing. Harmoniously blended

PRIMITIVE ANCIENT ROBES ARE JUXTAPOSED WITH LUXURIOUS CLOTHS such as silk and lace.

It really is the most fun job in fashion, but you have to give it 100 per cent to be successful.
JAANA JÄTYRI CEO AT TRENDSTOP.COM

WORST THINGS ABOUT THE JOB

Fashion is so fast now, and the high street is so quick to translate catwalk/fashion trends into affordable products, that it's become more difficult to predict trends. Also, trend information has become hugely accessible to all, and it's featured in many magazines and newspapers, which means that working as a forecaster you need to ensure you're always a few steps ahead.
HELEN BAKUNOWICZ, FREELANCE TREND FORECASTER

WHAT SKILLS ARE NEEDED TO BE A TREND FORECASTER?

- You need to live and breathe fashion and have a great 'eye' for spotting interesting things
- Excellent research skills — anything from studying the catwalk collections each season, researching the coolest blogs, reading all the latest fashion and lifestyle magazines, to photographing trends on the street
- Good photography skills — this is a big part of the job
- Strong writing skills are a bonus when putting presentations and reports together
- Being able to speak another language may be useful in dealing with overseas clients
- You should be confident at presentation — both verbally and when doing layouts

A good gut feeling also helps when faced with a decision of which trend is right; my rule is to follow your instincts. **RACHEL BANHAM, SENIOR TREND RESEARCHER AT TRENDSTOP.COM**

All images courtesy of Trendstop.com

Rachel is a Senior Researcher at London-based trend forecasting company Trendstop.com, where she has been employed since 2008. Prior to working with Trendstop.com, Rachel worked as a Senior Designer on womens and menswear for Red or Dead, Boxfresh and Pentland Brands. Read on to find out what Rachel's role involves working in trend forecasting.

EDUCATION
School subjects: Art, Craft, Design Technology, English, Maths, Science, Geography (plus two advanced GCSEs in Art and Photography)
A-levels: Art, Media Studies, English, General Studies
College: BTEC Diploma in Fashion & Textiles at Colchester School of Art & Design
University: BA degree in Fashion & Textiles at Colchester School of Art & Design

HOW DID YOU GET INTO TREND FORECASTING? When I was studying, I had a dream of getting into forecasting and started collecting trend magazines, taking inspiration from them while working on my projects. I knew it would be a hard industry to get into so I decided the best route would be to experience life as a designer first. I found it easier to get into once I had experience working in design, as some of our clients are designers so I know what information they need.

WHAT DOES YOUR JOB INVOLVE NOW? Each day is different but that's what makes my job interesting. My responsibilities include working on seasonal reports during the catwalk shows, working with the team on the close-to-season and forecast theme stories which we work on six and 18 months in advance, and covering key shapes. I work on both men's and women's forecasting – because I've worked on mens- and womenswear design, I have the experience to work on both genders.

WHAT SORT OF CLIENTS DO YOU WORK WITH? Clients range from stores/brands such as ASOS, New Look or Next to manufacturers, small design houses, stylists and celebrities.

WHAT METHODS DO YOU USE TO PREDICT TRENDS? We take a lot of inspiration from consumers (the trends people in everyday life are following), and we also take direction from the high-end designers and the catwalks each season.

WHERE ARE THE BEST PLACES FOR TREND SPOTTING, AND WHAT DO YOU ACTUALLY DO WHEN YOU'RE THERE? In London there are lots of good locations, such as Brick Lane, Hoxton and Portobello Road. The seasonal fashion weeks and music festivals are also great, as people are dressed up for the occasion and you get lots of people in one place. We take photos of things we think are interesting, and people are usually very flattered when we say their outfit is cool and ask for a picture.

ARE THE HOURS LONG? Yes, but when you enjoy your job like I do it doesn't feel like they are. We work 9.30am until 6pm, but working in the trend industry means you never really switch off as something always catches your eye wherever you are.

DO YOU GET NERVOUS BEFORE MAKING A TREND PRESENTATION? I don't have to do them in my current role, as my boss does them. In my previous role as a designer I used to get nervous when I started out, but the more you do them the easier it gets.

Industry Insider!

Rachel looks just like this in real life!

INTRO

The key to this theme lies in its modern re-invention. Emphasis is shifted from more obvious tribal prints and ethnic skirts of previous seasons onto subtler patterns and a greater emphasis on contemporary layering and appliqué.

On the Buffalo Trail mixes authentic Peruvian, Native American, Gipsy, Tibetan and Mongolian influences with the early 1980's Buffalo look pioneered by Vivienne Westwood's 'Nostalgia of Mud' collection and Bill Gibb's Peruvian inspired layering from the same period.

Dazed and Confused, September 2007

All images courtesy of Trendstop.com

Our experts have taken time out of their busy schedules to tell you what it's really like working in trend forecasting, and how you can prepare for a career in this sector. They include:

Jaana Jätyri: Based in London, Jaana is CEO of the leading trend forecasting company, Trendstop.com (www.trendstop.com). A real trend guru, she has worked in forecasting for over ten years, and her clients include everyone from high-street brands and retailers, celebrities and stylists, and e-tailers. Jaana graduated in 1999 from Central St. Martins with a first class honours degree in Fashion Design with Marketing. Prior to setting up Trendstop.com in 2002, Jaana worked as a digital design consultant for high-street companies.

Helen Bakunowicz: Helen is a freelance Trend & Colour Consultant based in London. She has over nine years of international experience and holds a BA (Hons) in Fashion Textiles with Business Studies. Her first role was textile designer with the Style Council in New York, before going on to be Head of Trend at Bureaux, a design consultancy in London. Helen is now Editor and Panelist for the International Colour Authority and also works for a diverse range of trend websites, high-street and supermarket brands as well as being a panelist for the British Textile Colour Group.

WHAT DOES AN AVERAGE DAY INVOLVE?

There are both office and field-based roles in trend forecasting. An office role would include visits to launches, press days, etc, but on the whole it involves working on the computer. Depending on your seniority level the tasks vary and include researching, compiling and editing trend stories, or assisting in these tasks. Field-based roles involve spotting trends through to writing and photography.
JAANA JÄTYRI

A typical day during the research period could involve assessing catwalks and analysing them by trend, colour and product category. Or visiting specialist book, magazine and fashion stores or galleries to see what's out there and worth talking about. I might be creating colour palettes for different brands and phasing them appropriately for the season, or attending a trade fair to feed back on.
HELEN BAKUNOWICZ

HOW DO YOU PREDICT TRENDS – WHAT'S THE PROCESS?

We receive a vast amount of data from our global trend spotters, who cover art, street style, boutiques, catwalks, vintage, launches. From our HQ, our team analyses it and puts it into different trends/themes. We also use information sourced from Twitter, Google, MySpace and Facebook, and use other market research to back up our findings. Our analysis is then presented on our website, and on mobile devices for clients to access.
JAANA JÄTYRI

I begin by looking at cultural information: events, movies, books, stores, exhibitions, music and catwalks. Based on this research I formulate themes and colour stories for the season. Working initially two years ahead means the themes at this point are fairly abstract, becoming more focused as we get closer to the season. About 12–18 months ahead we are able to analyse with more detail in terms of product. Not all trends are brand new – many are evolutionary rather than revolutionary – much of the process is about looking at timing and predicting the rise and peak of a trend.
HELEN BAKUNOWICZ

IS IT FUN HAVING CONTROL OVER WHAT PEOPLE WILL BE WEARING IN FUTURE?

Yes, absolutely. This is where the process begins, and it's great to be a part of it.
JAANA JÄTYRI

HOW DO YOU KNOW IF SOMETHING WILL BECOME A TREND?

One part is years of experience seeing seasons come and go, and noticing what looks new by comparison. Another part is well-developed gut instinct. The rest is analytical research to demonstrate the feasibility of a trend through statistics and data mining.
JAANA JÄTYRI

When you start to see repetition in what's coming through, it is clear that there is a trend building up. Thorough research and keeping your eyes and ears open is essential!
HELEN BAKUNOWICZ

IS THIS A DIFFICULT SECTOR OF THE INDUSTRY TO GET INTO?

What makes it difficult is that there are a huge number of applicants who want to work in forecasting, and only a small number of trend forecasting companies.
JAANA JÄTYRI

WHAT HAPPENS IF YOU GET IT WRONG? HAS THIS EVER HAPPENED?

Trend research is a form of market research, with a creative angle. We collate a lot of data to back up trends. As long as the research is well substantiated, the trend will most likely happen. If it changes direction, we update our analysis and inform our customers. Predicting when a trend is going to hit can be tricky, as trends can sometimes take longer to filter through to the masses than expected.
JAANA JÄTYRI

HOW LONG DOES IT TAKE TO GET PAID WORK?

Most companies suggest a three-month trial period which can be unpaid. However, some will take graduates in student placement roles and wait about six months before considering them for a permanent position if there is one available.
HELEN BAKUNOWICZ

WHAT SHOULD A WANNABE TREND FORECASTER HAVE IN THEIR PORTFOLIO?

Beautiful images, including ones that demonstrate good photography skills, attractive mood boards that show an ability to find new trends and build them into relevant themes, and good quality descriptive text; CAD drawings or Illustrator graphics are a bonus.
JAANA JÄTYRI

Creative mood boards identifying a trend with co-ordinating colour palettes, key shapes for the season, and catwalk analysis by trend and product category. A focused trend project would also be great, aimed towards a particular brand or retailer for an upcoming season.
HELEN BAKUNOWICZ

HOW MUCH TRAVEL DO YOU DO IN THIS SECTOR?

There can be a lot of travelling to trade fairs, stores or clients throughout the year. Typical cities for trade fairs would be Paris and Barcelona. Florence, Copenhagen, Berlin and New York are great for trend shopping.
HELEN BAKUNOWICZ

DO PEOPLE NEED TO HAVE A DEGREE TO WORK IN FORECASTING?

You need to have an in-depth knowledge of fashion

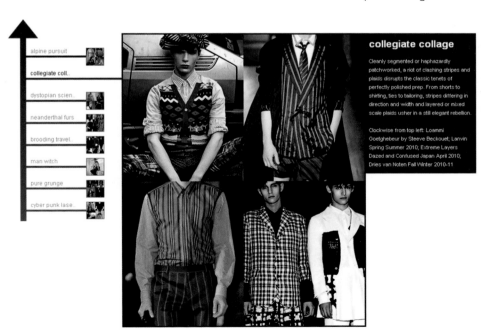

collegiate collage

Cleanly segmented or haphazardly patchworked, a riot of clashing stripes and plaids disrupts the classic tenets of perfectly polished prep. From shorts to shirting, ties to tailoring, stripes differing in direction and width and layered or mixed scale plaids usher in a still elegant rebellion.

Clockwise from top left: Loammi Goetghebeur by Steeve Beckouet; Lanvin Spring Summer 2010; Extreme Layers Dazed and Confused Japan April 2010; Dries van Noten Fall Winter 2010-11

alpine pursuit
collegiate coll..
dystopian scien..
neanderthal furs
brooding travel..
man witch
pure grunge
cyber punk lase..

All images courtesy of Trendstop.com

and the ability to spot a trend. The 13-year-old blogger Tavi, for example, has an in-depth knowledge of fashion, without having a degree. So it is possible to gain the required skills without one, but a degree course offers a more structured way to do this.
JAANA JÄTYRI

WHAT CAN I DO NOW TO BEGIN PREPARING FOR A CAREER IN FORECASTING?

If you're sure you want to work in forecasting, and you have the choice available, then it's a good idea to choose a specialist course. The next best options are a fashion design or journalism degree, but these don't offer complete training for trend forecasting. However, you can be proactive and seek additional ways to top up your skills. For example, you can boost your fashion design course knowledge by training yourself to write well, while you can boost a journalism degree by studying fashion history or Photoshop.
JAANA JÄTYRI

Start collecting information and begin seeing how everything links up; advertising with catwalks, fashion with film – it's all out there for you to see. Start a folder of things that inspire you – you need to become a sponge!
HELEN BAKUNOWICZ

HOW WOULD I GO ABOUT GETTING WORK EXPERIENCE ASSISTING IN A TREND FORECASTING STUDIO?

You need to write a professional covering letter, prepare a neat and presentable CV and create a portfolio to showcase your work. As well as good organisational skills, we would be looking for fashion knowledge and writing skills, ability to find and present trends, Photoshop/Illustrator skills, and ability to create attractive graphics. We might get 500 CVs a month, so your work needs to be good to stand out.
JAANA JÄTYRI

WILL TREND AGENCIES TAKE PEOPLE ON FOR WORK EXPERIENCE WHO ARE STILL AT HIGH SCHOOL?

The reason it's difficult to get a placement before university is because employers want to see that the person has made a commitment to follow a career in their industry. One way to try to prove yourself to an employer is by starting a blog or Twitter page that showcases your knowledge, like Tavi has done.
JAANA JÄTYRI

Yes – for short periods I've worked with high-school students. Even though the work experience is less hands-on at this level, it's really beneficial to be in the work environment and feel the atmosphere.
HELEN BAKUNOWICZ

navajo sport

ice congo
old lady rebell..
cyber punk lase..
90s corinne day..
masculine linge..
milanese tea ro..
beige lounge
futuristic eliz..
pol chambost co..
renaissance met..
tribal skin paint

navajo sport

A further indication of cross cultural hybridity, Navajo nuances adorn all American sportswear. A compliment to classic grey jersey; feathers, beading, hessian fabrication and Pendleton prints pitch athleticism into native territory.

Clockwise from top left: William Rast Fall Winter 2010-11; Jalouse April 2010 Jalouse Beauty; William Rast Fall Winter 2010-11; Teen Vogue July 2009

All images courtesy of Trendstop.com

To Do List

▶ **LOOK** at as many websites and blogs as you can relating to trends, colour and forecasting, so you can begin to get an idea of how information is presented in the industry, both visually and in written formats. Most of the agency sites have sections you can only access if you're a paying client, but some have areas anyone can look at. Helen Bakunowicz recommends the following sites: www.stylesight.com / www.wgsn.com / www.mudpie.co.uk / www.thecoolhunter.co.uk / www.colourlovers.com

"You can download our free TrendTracker mobile app by going to **www.mobile. trendstop.com** from your phone's browser. Our blog at **www.blog.trendstop.com** and Twitter page **www.twitter.com/trendstop** include snippets of our daily trend sightings."
JAANA JÄTYRI

Another cool site is: **www.letscolourproject.com**

▶ **PRACTISE** your photography and observation skills. Carry a camera and notebook wherever you go and jot down anything you think could be an emerging trend. Take photos of people when you're out and about (ask their permission first). Like the trend forecasters featured in this chapter, next time you're at a festival, gig or party watch out for interesting looks. Don't focus on things everyone is wearing already (they will already be a trend), instead look for people who are wearing interesting things or have styled themselves in a certain way. These could be the trends of the future.

▶ **PREPARE** a portfolio for either work experience interviews or to get into fashion college. Start to gather all your research, photos, notes, etc, into relevant themes or 'stories' and put into a sketch book. Then choose the most exciting and interesting parts to develop into final boards of work (presented on A3 pieces of card, which is a good size to work on). Think about how to get your message or theme across visually and with small amounts of text — you could include photos, postcards, coloured paper, magazine/newspaper cut-outs, fabrics, trims, buttons and drawings. Make sure the end result looks as neat and professional as possible — presentation is everything in trend forecasting.

CHAPTER FOUR: STYLING

IN THIS CHAPTER:

"Don't give up easily. It's tiring, but you'll get there in the end!"

Polly Errington, Stylist

Photographer: Stefano Brunesci / Stylist: Polly Errington

WHAT DOES A STYLIST DO?

The role of a fashion stylist involves creating a series of key 'looks' based on a theme or brief given by a client. Their job is to make the individual they are working with look as good as possible, or often to dramatically change a person's look, depending on the requirements of their client. Stylists are responsible for deciding on clothes, footwear, accessories and props, but they may also decide on the location if working on a photo shoot. There is lots of fun and creativity involved in coming up with new looks, but there are also duller aspects to the job, such as ironing, making small alterations, lugging suitcases of garments around, and lots of waiting around on jobs. Most stylists start out as assistants, and can work their way up to senior level or, in magazine work, to become fashion directors.

WHO EMPLOYS STYLISTS?

Most stylists are self-employed and work on a freelance basis – it's unusual to work full-time for a company unless employed by a magazine or newspaper as a fashion director or fashion assistant. Stylists work on a diverse range of jobs, including shoots for magazines and newspapers (editorial), styling for catwalk shows, personal image consultancy for individuals (including celebrities), commercial jobs for advertising, and styling on music videos, TV and films.

KEY WORKING RELATIONSHIPS

It's rare for stylists to work completely alone. Apart from working directly with their models, the majority of stylists form part of a team on each job – the end result depends on ideas and input from lots of different people. The team might include a make-up artist, hair stylist, photographer, fashion designer or creative director, as well as various assistants.

RELATED ROLES

Apart from the types of styling mentioned above, some people may also work as personal shoppers for private clients (combining this with wardrobe consultations) or within department stores and boutiques, where they will be responsible for putting together new looks for a customer such as for a wedding or special occasion. Another role related to – but not strictly the same as – styling, is that of image consultant. This involves analysing a client's whole look, including their body language and overall presentation as well as their clothes.

WORKING HOURS

This isn't a 9–5 job – most of the stylists we spoke to emphasised that they have to take work whenever it comes up, and no two days are the same. Stylists have to be very flexible and willing to work long hours, often with early starts and including weekends and holidays. There is no average pattern to the working week, as it differs so much from person to person.

SALARY

The majority of stylists work for free when they start out and it can take time to build up to paid work. This can be approximately £50 – £75 a day for assistants, leading to anything between £100 and £500+ a day for experienced stylists.

Photographer Alex Leonhardt / Stylist: Polly Errington

EDUCATION:

- Useful school/college subjects: Art, Business Studies, English, Textiles, Media Studies, Photography

While qualifications are not essential (remember that your portfolio is more important than anything else) here are some specialist courses to consider:
- London College of Fashion – Foundation Degree Fashion Styling & Photography
- UCA (Epsom) – BA (Hons) Fashion Promotion & Imaging
- Kirklees College (Yorkshire) – Foundation Degree Fashion Styling & Promotion

BEST THINGS ABOUT THE JOB

- Going to fashion shows and meeting the designers is always fun
- It allows you to be creative, and you meet so many interesting people
- It's exciting as there's something new on every shoot
- The freebies are great

WORST THINGS ABOUT THE JOB

- The long hours! There's lots of standing around and waiting– for the photographer to finish testing the lighting, and hair and make-up to finish their work – before you can put the models in their outfits
- Waiting for payment from clients (it can take ages to get paid)
- Lots of running around picking up garments from designers and PR companies
- Being responsible for expensive clothing – it's very stressful when you have to look after a £2,000 dress and make sure it doesn't get marked with make-up, or the model doesn't sweat all over it. That's what insurance is for, but it's still a nightmare

Photographer: Stefano Brunesci / Stylist: Polly Errington

WHAT SKILLS ARE NEEDED TO BE A FASHION STYLIST?
- A love for all things fashion
- An eye for detail
- Being able to visualise the outcome of a shoot
- You should be sociable, approachable and organised – this is very important if you want to get ahead quickly
- Punctuality – you should be flexible and always on time
- An understanding of photography, make-up and hair is always a good thing but you'll pick this up along the way
- You need to know how to fit garments to a model, so practise hemming and pinning
- Knowledge of fashion trends and forecasting

With seven years in the industry, Polly Errington is a freelance stylist based in London working mainly on editorial (magazine fashion features) for publications such as *Flair*, *Anglomania*, and *L'ag*. Additional work includes commercial advertising campaigns plus runway shows at London Fashion Week. Polly took time out from her busy schedule to answer questions on what it's REALLY like to work in styling.

EDUCATION
GCSEs: English, Science, Maths, Art, Design & Technology, IT, French, Geography
A-levels: Business Studies, English and Art
Degree: BA in European Fashion at the Kent Institute of Art & Design (now UCCA)

IS WORKING IN STYLING AS YOU EXPECTED IT TO BE?

No. It looks and sounds glamorous, but it isn't always. If you get paid to work on some amazing location then that's great, but it doesn't happen often. I've been freezing in a dirty warehouse while pinning a massive dress to a model; that was probably the worst. One of the more fun jobs was an underwater shoot. Styling that was a challenge, but the results were great so well worth the effort.

WHERE DO YOU GET THE INSPIRATION FOR YOUR SHOOTS?

Sometimes the obvious such as fashion magazines, but I can also get inspiration from some random girl with a striking outfit sitting opposite me on the train. Sometimes inspiration strikes when I just start daydreaming, or I can start brainstorming and ideas just start tumbling out one after the other. It's handy to have my iPhone so I can send myself an email with my latest ideas. Inspiration can come from anywhere.

HOW MUCH CREATIVE FREEDOM DO YOU HAVE ON EACH SHOOT – WHO MAKES THE MAJOR DECISIONS?

Stylists often have a lot of creative freedom and I regularly direct the hair and make-up. The photographer or art director tends to run things, but the stylist's opinion is always very valid. I get involved and assist the photographer with directing the poses and facial expressions.

WHAT'S BEEN YOUR FAVOURITE STYLING JOB AND WHY?

Probably the underwater shoot for the National Childbirth Trust. I styled a pregnant woman with lots of beautiful flowing dresses, which looked amazing in water. Plus I got to splash around in a really warm pool all day long!

WHAT HAS BEEN YOUR WORST STYLING JOB AND WHY?

A shoot I did in a nightclub in Wales. The make-up artist did the opposite of what the client wanted, the model was a prima donna, and an expensive silk dress was dumped in a pool of bright blue liquid soap. A very stressful and long day.

HOW DO YOU GO ABOUT FINDING NEW JOBS?

Jobs tend to come to me now that I have so many contacts. But when I started out I used to network like crazy. It's all about making contacts and helping each other out. Getting an agent is what you should aim for, as they can find work on your behalf.

HOW MUCH DID YOU GET PAID WHEN YOU STARTED OUT?

Nothing! But you can't expect to get paid if you have no experience. Once I started to build up my portfolio, I began to get enquiries and my travel would be paid. After that I would get about £50 to style a shoot. It's hard getting clothing loaned to you if you have no credentials. It takes time, but networking and meeting up with designers will get you far.

HOW LONG DOES IT TAKE TO BEGIN TO GET PAID WORK?

It depends on how good you are and how much you network. It took me about a year of working for free before I got my first big paid job.

DO YOU GET PAID ON A DAY RATE OR PROJECT RATE?

I charge a day rate, plus prep fees (for liaising with the designer or PR agencies and collecting the garments).

Polly in her pink flamingo glasses

Industry Insider!

You never know if a project will finish when it's supposed to, so you could sell yourself short if you charge a project rate.

WHAT DOES AN AVERAGE DAY INVOLVE?

If I'm working on a shoot it normally involves getting up early, checking that all of the clothes are packed, and then travelling to the location. Most work is in London — it's a nightmare to transport everything we need on the Tube. Once we arrive I set up the clothes on a rail, then my assistant and I either iron or steam them so they look pristine. Once the photographer starts shooting, we keep an eye on everything. I often bring a dressing gown for the model in case they get cold, or to cover them up if they're feeling exposed.

When we've finished shooting I pack — I have a checklist to make sure I haven't forgotten anything (and also to make sure no one has pinched anything — sadly it does happen). Days when I'm not shooting usually involve running around London collecting samples or emailing designers and agencies to ask them to loan me items (that's called sending out a press request when you're styling for a magazine).

"It looks and sounds glamorous but it isn't always like that!"

Polly Errington, Stylist

Photographer: Stefano Brunesci / Stylist: Polly Errington

We've put your questions on styling to a team of industry insiders who all have relevant experience working in this sector. Our experts include:

Madeleine Østlie — Freelance Fashion Assistant & Stylist
Among others, Madeleine works for *Twin Magazine*, Kate Phelan (a director at British *Vogue*) and Lulu Kennedy, founder of Fashion East. She completed a BA in Fashion Merchandising at the University of Westminster and worked in buying at Topshop Head Office for three years, before leaving to pursue a career in styling full time. You can see Madeleine's work on her blog: www.seamlessfashion.blogspot.com

Mhairi Gibb — Freelance Stylist
Beginning her career as a fashion assistant at *Dazed & Confused* and *Another Magazine*, Mhairi went on to assist Katy England for more than three years. She is now an established stylist with more than eight years of experience and has contributed to publications such as *Amelia's Magazine*, *Tank* and *Vogue Homme*, and carried out a wealth of advertising and video styling work. Mhairi has a BA in Fashion Marketing from the University of Northumbria. You can see some of her work at: www.mhairigibb.com

Polly Errington — Freelance Stylist
London-based Polly works on a freelance basis and has experience in editorial, commercial, advertising and runway. Her clients have included *L'ag*, *Anglomania*, *Flair*, *Kult* and *Living North*. She also has experience in personal shopping and retail management. Polly holds a BA in European Fashion from the Kent Institute of Art & Design (now UCA). Check out her work at: www.pollyerrington.co.uk

HOW CAN I PREPARE FOR A CAREER IN STYLING WHILE I'M STILL AT SCHOOL OR COLLEGE?

Get as much work experience as you can within the industry. This could range from working in retail, in press offices, with designers or a fashion events company, dressing back stage at a show, etc.
You make so many contacts when you do this — sometimes it's not what you know, it's who you know.
MHAIRI GIBB

WHAT DOES AN ASSISTANT DO ON WORK EXPERIENCE?

It really depends on where and whom you're working for. Usually if you spend your placement as a fashion assistant at a magazine you'll be working under the fashion director and/or editor. You would be responsible for calling in clothes for the upcoming shoots, liaising with press offices in London, Milan, Paris and New York. These clothes would be your responsibility and you would be expected to look after them. Sometimes it would also be down to you to source specific things for a shoot, like jewellery or accessories. You would then, it's hoped, get to assist the editor directly on the shoot. And when the shoot is finally over it's your responsibility to get all the clothes back to the press offices. This can be done by courier or quite often on foot!
MHAIRI GIBB

IS IT HARD TO GET WORK EXPERIENCE IN STYLING?

No, but you have to show and prove you are truly passionate about the job. And you have to accept that much work is unpaid for a while.
MADELEINE ØSTLIE

I think these days it's a lot more competitive so more people are competing for the one place. Most magazines will have more than one placement at a time that can last from a week to a couple of months. If you're lucky you might then be taken on by one of the fashion editors or stylists as their full-time assistant.
MHAIRI GIBB

HOW DO I CONTACT STYLISTS TO GET WORK EXPERIENCE WITH THEM?

In order to get work experience, it is best to approach idependent magazines that are not run by a big publishing house, and that often need more help.
MADELEINE ØSTLIE

If you don't have a direct contact for them or their current assistant, email the fashion department of the magazine they work for or email their agent with your CV and images of work. These are always easy to find online and the majority of senior stylists will be represented by an agent. Follow it up with a phone call

Stylist: Cat Watson / Photographer: Keith Clouston

to introduce yourself or try to arrange a meeting.
MHAIRI GIBB

HAVE YOU EVER WORKED WITH GARMENTS YOU DIDN'T LIKE? IF SO, HOW DID YOU DEAL WITH THIS SITUATION?

You constantly work with garments you don't like. It's best to keep your opinions to yourself, unless you are asked, when you can then articulately and politely explain why you think a particular piece isn't right. Stylists and photographers do not like false opinions. Honesty is always the best policy but you have to know when it's right to share your opinion.
MADELEINE ØSTLIE

WHO IS THE MOST FAMOUS PERSON YOU'VE STYLED, AND WHAT WAS THE EXPERIENCE LIKE?

I wouldn't really like to name drop, but there's been a few. It's pretty nerve-racking but, of course, they're just normal people like you or I.
MHAIRI GIBB

WHAT ARE YOUR ESSENTIALS WHEN WORKING ON A SHOOT?

Toupee tape, pins, masking tape, a steamer and an iron.
POLLY ERRINGTON

WHAT IS THE BEST JOB TO WORK ON: MAGAZINES, RUNWAY OR VIDEOS?

All of the above. Not one is better than the other, and each magazine, show and shoot varies so much you can't generalise like that.
MADELEINE ØSTLIE

Personally I love runway the most. It's very intense in the run-up to the show and sometimes you can work with little or no sleep but the adrenaline keeps you going.
MHAIRI GIBB

IS IT ESSENTIAL TO HAVE A DEGREE TO WORK IN STYLING?

No, you may be better off starting assisting and interning once you leave school. However, it's hard work and not right for everyone.
MADELEINE ØSTLIE

WHAT ARE YOUR TOP TIPS FOR THOSE LOOKING TO GET INTO STYLING?

Make lots and lots of friends in the fashion industry — the more people you know, the easier it will be to find work. Be picky. Don't work with just anyone. I've seen loads of people who will work on any shoot, but might get bad quality images in return for all their hard work. Research the team you want to work with, and make sure that you will all benefit equally from each other. And don't give up easily. It's tiring, but you'll get there in the end.
POLLY ERRINGTON

HOW MUCH, ON AVERAGE, DOES A STYLIST EARN?

Some fashion assistants work for nearly nothing; one magazine in particular pays them as little as £4,000 a YEAR! Many assistants often have two jobs or get support from their families to survive. At the other end of the scale, some top stylists can get more than £5,000 a day.
MADELEINE ØSTLIE

WHAT SHOULD A WANNABE STYLIST HAVE IN THEIR PORTFOLIO?

Images that show your best work only — it's all about quality not quantity. You should include a range of shoots showing how diverse your talent is — for example, swimwear, winter woollies, something 'high' fashion; not necessarily designer names, but a shoot with a kick to it (interesting angles, crazy hair or make-up).
POLLY ERRINGTON

HOW DO YOU FIND NEW PROJECTS TO WORK ON?

A lot of it is about collaborating with other creatives, which could be designers, photographers, art directors or even make-up artists. You're always on the lookout for new inspiration. It might be that you pitch an idea to a publication or someone commissions you to do a shoot for them. It's always good to keep networking.
MHAIRI GIBB

Stylist: Mhairi Gibb / Photographer: Gemma Booth

THIS SHOOT WAS FOR *AMELIA'S MAGAZINE*

Photographer Gemma Booth and I had talked about doing something together for a while. Her work is always young and playful and she loves to shoot outside with natural light. We came up with the Trick or Treat story by taking inspiration from old '70s pictures of kids dressing up for Halloween and Gala Days, together with looks from the collections from that season, and characters I made up.

The clothes were a mixture of vintage, high street and designer ranging from Camden Market to Alexander McQueen. Some I made myself like a mummy outfit which was basically tights and pieces of elastic. We shot it in a little village in Essex — the houses had been built in the '60s/ '70s so it worked perfectly with what we were doing. There were lots of quirky little elements to it like the orange cat hanging off the roof of the garage and the Easter Island-type mini statues.

I love shooting on location as it always has such a different dynamic to the studio, you work more closely as a team.

MHAIRI GIBB

Stylist: Mhairi Gibb / Photographer: Gemma Booth

To Do List

▶ **RESEARCH** the work of other stylists to see how they present their images and to get inspiration – check out online portfolios on sites such as **www.iqons.com** / **www.nineteen74.com** / **www.whoistesting.com** / **www.fashioncontest.com**

▶ **CREATE A PORTFOLIO – YOU WON'T BE TAKEN SERIOUSLY WITHOUT IT** You will need a portfolio containing images of your work, whether you're applying for a place at college/uni, or trying to find work experience or paid employment.

You can do this by working on test shoots to practise your skills; this will involve creating a series of key 'looks' or themes with a team of people including a photographer, make-up artist, hair stylist and model. If you're at college you should make friends with students from beauty, hair-styling and photography courses, who will also be interested in developing their portfolio, so you can build up a team of people to work with on shoots.

▶ **GET SOME WORK EXPERIENCE** While it's great to gain experience working on a major magazine or runway show, remember that this type of work is hard to get and very competitive. Alternatives include working on local magazines or newspapers – most cities and large towns will have a newspaper or 'lifestyle' magazine with a small fashion section, where you might be able to help out on shoots. If you want to style for the catwalk, it's worth offering assistance at local charity/school/college fashion shows.

▶ **GET A WEEKEND JOB** It's useful to build up experience within a related field – working in a designer clothing or department store can give you knowledge of creating looks and the ability to interact with customers. Look out for stores in your area that offer a personal shopping service.

▶ **READ** as many fashion magazines as possible to keep up to date with trends and styling ideas.

▶ **DEVELOP** your collection of props and garments to use on test shoots. Shop in charity shops, car boot sales, on Ebay, at flea markets – there's no need to spend a lot. Borrow clothes from friends and family to use on shoots if you don't have any money to buy things (but look after everything well).

'Set up your own blog to show prospective employers images of work from any shoots you've been on.'
MADELEINE ØSTLIE

INFORM   INSPIRE   IDEAS   INNOVATE   IMAGINATION

TEXTILES | INTERIORS | FASHION

YshLondon (pronounced 'eesh') is a **free textile, fashion and interiors online magazine**, offering students, young designers and businesses the latest news and trends happening in London.

interview:
We interview key industry figures, from the Selfridges window display team to leading trend forecasters, at home or at their studio, outlining career paths and advice to students and young graduates.

inspiration:
We report from important design exhibitions, trade shows, all the key graduate shows and London stores at the forefront of design.

trends:
We present street photography, with monthly key trend analysis from London, Paris, Berlin, New York, and Tokyo.

It's now FREE to signup! Simply go to **www.yshlondon.com** to join us today!

careers:
We offer a dedicated careers and jobs page - useful tips on the dos and don'ts of applying for that job/work placement/course, CV clinics and portfolio advice.

knowledge:
All our reporters have trained in fashion, textiles or design and are currently working in the industry as designers, trend forecasters and fashion journalists. They have been there and done that – they know their stuff!

We provide a one stop shop, from the comfort of your laptop, for all that is textiles, fashion and interiors in and around the city. We look forward to welcoming you onboard!

For more details, email us at **info@yshlondon.com** or just give us a call on **020 7580 4227**.

IN THIS CHAPTER:

"When I'm sitting opposite Kate Moss at a fashion show I completely miss all the clothes on the runway for staring at her!"

Lucy Wood, Fashion News Editor, *Look* Magazine

WHAT DOES A FASHION JOURNALIST DO?

It is the job of a fashion journalist to communicate what is happening within the fashion industry to a wide audience, often at both a national and international level. This involves feature writing (editorial), producing trend and catwalk reports, putting together designer profiles and conducting and writing fashion or beauty product reviews. Apart from the actual writing part, journalists spend a lot of time organising and styling shoots, visiting designers and fashion companies (on press days, where they preview the new collections), and attending fashion shows, events and parties, in order to keep ahead of all the latest news and gossip.

WHO EMPLOYS FASHION JOURNALISTS?

Most journalists work for print publications – magazines and newspapers. Those working on magazines can choose between the consumer press – magazines written for the general public, such as *LOOK*, *Vogue*, *Grazia*, *Elle*, etc – or the trade press, which involves producing articles for other people who work in the fashion business on industry news, reports and events. Examples of these include *Drapers*, *Retail Week* and *WWD*. There are also growing opportunities for journalists to work in digital media, such as online magazines and websites, and additionally for trend forecasting agencies and TV production companies. Many people in fashion journalism are self-employed, working on a freelance basis, contributing articles to lots of different publications.

KEY WORKING RELATIONSHIPS:

Every publication is slightly different, but the average team at a print magazine involves several desks or departments, including Pictures, Features, News, Art, Subs, Beauty, Fashion, Web and 'Top Table' (where the top, top editors sit). Each team has junior and senior staff, ranging from interns, fashion and editorial assistants, writers, and editors and directors. In addition to their direct colleagues, journalists will liaise with PR and marketing agencies, designers, stylists, contributors and model agencies.

RELATED ROLES:

It's not uncommon for fashion journalists to come from other sectors of the industry once they have a few years of experience, such as design, styling, PR and marketing.

WORKING HOURS:

Journalism is well known as an industry where the hours can be very long and overtime is common, especially before a deadline. Lucy Wood from *LOOK* explains: 'Some days are a standard 9 to 5 but you have to always be prepared to stay late at the drop of a hat or dash off to a launch or event with just five minutes to touch up your make-up.'

SALARY:

Pay is quite low in journalism, with entry-level salaries approximately £15k. The average fashion editor can expect anything between £30k and £60k+, with uber-editors (such as Anna Wintour from American *Vogue*) likely to be on much more.

FASHION EDITOR
LONDON FASHION EDITOR LUCY WOOD OPENS UP HER NOTEBOOK

FRIDAY, 7 MAY 2010
Vintage Chanel Handbags at Amelie Boutique

Red quilted tote, £1500 vintage Chanel circa 1986 - 1988 at Amelie Boutique

ABOUT ME

FASHION EDITOR
Fashion Editor is fashion insider Lucy Wood's online notebook. From the latest 'It' handbags, product launches, parties and fashion weeks to red carpet press releases, collection previews and Topshop's new must-haves - it's all here on her live-from-the-fashion-desk daily blog. Contact Fashion Editor at fashioneditor@hotmail.com
VIEW MY COMPLETE PROFILE

LUCY WOOD'S PORTFOLIO
Visit Fashion-Editor-Portfolio.blogspot.com **for more information about Fashion Editor Lucy Wood**

wikipedia.org/wiki/Lucy_Wood

twitter.com/FashionNewsEd

ADDTHIS
Share
(Search Fashion Editor)

FOLLOW MY TWEETS
follow me on Twitter

BLOG ARCHIVE
▼ 2010 (91)

EDUCATION:

Useful school/college subjects: Art & Design, English, Media Studies, Business Studies, Journalism, Fashion, Textiles

Although it's not essential to have studied journalism (many people come from a different sector), there are specialist courses to consider:
- UCA Epsom: BA (Hons) Fashion Journalism
- London College of Fashion: BA (Hons) Fashion Journalism (Print, Broadcast)
- Southampton Solent University: BA (Hons) Writing Fashion & Culture

BEST THINGS ABOUT THE JOB

- Every day is a shopping day
- Great discount cards for stores
- There's an endless supply of new brands to be discovered
- Free beauty products – I haven't bought shampoo for years

LUCY WOOD, FASHION NEWS EDITOR, *LOOK* MAGAZINE

WORST THINGS ABOUT THE JOB

- You're never going to be rich unless you become famous, like Gok Wan
- Fierce competition for jobs
- Long hours
- It's a lifestyle, not just a job – it takes over everything
- There's no eye candy in the office – it's 95 per cent female

LUCY WOOD, FASHION NEWS EDITOR, *LOOK* MAGAZINE

Page from Lucy's blog

LUCY WOOD OUTLINES THE SKILLS NEEDED TO BE A FASHION JOURNALIST:

- A good eye and the ability to edit rails and rails of great clothes down to about 10 pieces a page
- Knowing the dictionary inside out
- It goes without saying that you should have excellent writing and communication skills, and also be able to spell
- Confidence and excellent social skills – you can't be shy in this profession

Image: Shutterstock Images LLC

Lucy Wood works for the leading UK fashion magazine, *LOOK*, where she's held the title of Fashion News Editor for the past two and a half years. She manages the fashion news team and her role involves styling, writing, organising shoots, research, press appointments and, by her own admission, lots of shopping! Lucy was lucky enough to begin her career with *Grazia* magazine while still at uni, and also edited style publication *Random* (www.random-magazine.com) for a year alongside her job at *LOOK*. She now runs her own fashion blog in addition to her full-time role, which you can see at www.fashion-editor.com. Read on to find out how Lucy got to where she is now.

Industry Insider!

EDUCATION
School: English Language, Art & Design, Media Studies, Maths, Statistics, English Language, French, Science, Food Technology, RE, Cultural Studies
College: Fine Art, Media Studies, Graphic Products and Cultural Studies
University: BA (Hons) Fashion Journalism at the London College of Fashion

WHAT MADE YOU GO INTO FASHION INSTEAD OF MAINSTREAM JOURNALISM?

It started at college. We were being hassled to start applying to universities and, to be completely honest, I didn't know what I wanted to do or where I wanted to go. I scanned the UCAS website, skimming over all of the courses that to me sounded dull, and then the Fashion Journalism course popped up at the London College of Fashion and it dawned on me how much I had an interest in magazines and shopping. I was doing a part-time job at Karen Millen at the time and was heavily involved with the trend element of the job and it just felt right. It was the only course I applied for and I told myself that, if I didn't get in, I wouldn't go to university full stop. Thank goodness they accepted my application! Fashion is something I know inside out and that's why I didn't go down the mainstream journalism route.

IS WORKING IN FASHION JOURNALISM AS YOU EXPECTED IT TO BE?

It's exactly what I hoped it would be but I think people really underestimate the hard-graft element to it. Hours are long, it's fast-paced and highly competitive. You have to work hard at the start to be recognised by a fashion team. The only route in is through work experience, and there are hundreds of girls and boys who have months of work placements on their CV – they will always get first pick when it comes to a job opening on a fashion desk.

HOW LONG DID IT TAKE TO GET TO WHERE YOU ARE NOW AND HOW DID YOU GET THERE?

I was extremely lucky, and hard work coupled with being in the right place at the right time meant I had a bit of a fast track. While studying for my degree I went to *Grazia* on a two-week work placement and it soon became apparent that the magazine was going to be a great success, and I could see the potential for new jobs as the fashion team grew. I asked the Fashion Co-ordinator if I could come in each Friday (my one day off uni a week) to help her and did that for a few weeks. I only did the prices at first but it was a foot in the door.

Eventually the Fashion Editor asked me which direction I wanted to go in and I said fashion features. She introduced me to the Fashion News and Features Editor and that was it – she didn't have an assistant so I made myself hers. It was a case of making myself indispensable, and it worked. By the time it was the last year of my degree I was working at *Grazia* full-time – my course tutor knew my editor and knew I was in great hands and learning lots more than in the lecture hall. I did my dissertation from the *Grazia* office and turned into a sponge, taking as much from the experience as I could.

My editor, Melanie Rickey, taught me everything I know about fashion journalism and for that I owe her the world. By the time I was graduating my current job had come up and I applied and got it. It was like a dream – a degree and a job as *LOOK*'s Fashion News Editor overnight!

WHAT DOES AN AVERAGE DAY INVOLVE? First thing, before I've even opened my inbox, I read all the newspapers with a cup of tea. Next, I go through all the new paparazzi pictures that have come in overnight and spot emerging trends. As e-mails start coming in (I get about 200 a day) I plan what the team will be working on for the day and delegate pages. Then it's on to calling in product, styling up pages, press appointments and writing articles. If I'm lucky I'll squeeze some lunch in somewhere along the way.

WHERE DO YOU FIND INSPIRATION FOR YOUR ARTICLES? Blogs and US fashion sites are a great starting point. Then I start looking at the red carpet styles and then watch the cool LA starlets wearing their off-duty outfits. The style magazines such as *LOVE* and *V* are great for kooky trends too.

WHO HAS BEEN THE MOST INTERESTING PERSON YOU'VE MET FROM THE FASHION WORLD? Alexander Wang. He did a talk at Selfridges when he launched his concession there, and I was completely blown away. He's super young and has done so much in such a short space of time — to have become as big as he is in a tiny timescale is utterly inspiring. Love him!

WHAT FASHION-RELATED STORY HAS SHOCKED YOU THE MOST IN YOUR CAREER? Probably the size zero phenomenon. There was a time, for about six months, a couple of years ago when I couldn't pick up my phone for fear of being hounded by newspaper journalists wanting a quote on what I thought about size zero. It seems to have calmed down a bit now but, when the topic first appeared in the UK, it was like the world and his wife blamed fashion magazines for it.

WHICH FASHION ARTICLE ARE YOU MOST PROUD OF OR HAVE YOU ENJOYED THE MOST? There's not one specific article, but I'm most proud of all the new labels I've discovered and introduced to UK readers. It's sort of my niche — I always want to be first to unearth a new brand.

DO YOU EVER GET SHY OR NERVOUS AROUND FAMOUS DESIGNERS OR CELEBRITIES? You have to keep the professional head on but when I met Christian Louboutin my knees literally went weak. When I'm sitting opposite Kate Moss at a fashion show I completely miss all the clothes on the runway for staring at her!

ARE YOU IN AN OFFICE MOST OF THE TIME OR DO YOU GET TO GO OUT AND ABOUT? Mostly I'm in the office. I'd love to get out and about more but it just doesn't happen on a weekly mag. Breakfast and lunch appointments with PRs help, as they're a treat and break up the day. Travel is mainly in London but twice a year all of the editors flock to New York, Milan and Paris for the shows.

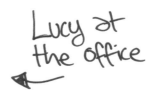

Lucy at the office

Portrait of Lucy Wood: Alistair Guy

Lucy Wood, Fashion News Editor at *LOOK* magazine (read our interview with her on the previous page), is joined by Kate Carter to answer all your questions on getting into fashion journalism.

Kate Carter: Kate is Editor of the Life & Style section of the *Guardian* website, covering articles on fashion, beauty, health, family, relationships and lots more. She took an unorthodox route into journalism, beginning her career working on television documentaries – as a Researcher, Assistant Producer, and then Producer/Director, before moving to work for the *Guardian* in 2007.

HOW MUCH OF YOUR JOB IS WRITING, AND WHAT DO YOU DO FOR THE REST OF THE TIME?

As I'm an editor I commission more than I write. I write our weekly fashion e-mail, Fashion Statement. So only a small proportion of my job is actually writing – the rest is commissioning, editing the site, planning ahead and trying to come up with new and exciting projects.
KATE CARTER

I'd say it's 40 per cent writing and 60 per cent calling in product, styling it up and shooting it. If I answered every e-mail that came into my inbox it would be 100 per cent e-mailing and not a lot else, so you learn to prioritise. My motto is that, if someone really needs to get hold of me, they have my mobile number and can call.
LUCY WOOD

WHAT ADVICE CAN YOU GIVE TO A BUDDING FASHION JOURNALIST?

Try and get as much experience as you can. When you find yourself at a busy magazine/paper/website, try to be as cheerful and helpful as possible. You might not get to write or do anything very exciting, but people will be impressed with you if you are willing to get stuck in and help with any task.
KATE CARTER

Start doing work experience every half-term and holiday. Although many mags do have a strict over-18s policy, still express your interest early. Know your topic inside out – know what is on the high street, know who's on the cover of magazines, read blogs and start to style your friends asap – practice makes perfect.
LUCY WOOD

WHAT IS THE BEST WAY TO APPROACH TRYING TO FIND WORK EXPERIENCE FOR FASHION MAGAZINES OR NEWSPAPERS?

Many magazines or newspapers have an official application procedure, so of course make sure you do that. But it also doesn't hurt to send personalised e-mails with your CV to people you particularly admire/want to work with – showing them you know what they do and how you might be able to help can only impress.
KATE CARTER

Usually the editorial assistant or fashion assistant will oversee all work experience candidates. It's best not to hassle the editors – they're so busy they just won't find the time to e-mail you back. Include the dates you are available to work and make sure there are no spelling mistakes – it really bugs us when there are. Recently a girl left her CV at the *LOOK* tent at the Isle of Wight festival – it was in a bucket and spade with lots of beauty treats and festival-related goodies. She'd made such an effort we just had to e-mail her, as it really caught our attention.
LUCY WOOD

HOW COMPETITIVE IS IT IN YOUR PROFESSION?

It is extremely competitive. Not just in fashion journalism but journalism generally – so be flexible. Don't just decide there is only one role that will do for you. Think of the future too. I work online and, when I was at school, jobs like mine didn't even exist.
KATE CARTER

Extremely. There's always someone lurking in the shadows waiting to snap up your job!
LUCY WOOD

IS THE INDUSTRY REALLY LIKE ITS PORTRAYAL IN FILMS LIKE *THE DEVIL WEARS PRADA*?

Not in our office, that's for sure!
KATE CARTER

IS YOUR JOB GLAMOROUS OR NOT?

That rather depends on what you think is glamorous. I'm sure it sounds amazing to go to fashion shows, but once you've queued yet again for another show that's running hideously late and you've got a deadline and you haven't had a chance to eat in eight hours — well, not so much. Of course there are some great things that we get to do as part of our jobs, but there is a lot of hard work too.

KATE CARTER

Yes! There are private jets, swanky restaurants, the Oscars and VIP everything but then you go home and eat beans on toast for dinner and realise that you're not a billionaire after all!

LUCY WOOD

WHEN ATTENDING CATWALK SHOWS, I FIND IT HARD TO CLEARLY SEE WHAT FABRICS AND TECHNIQUES ARE BEING USED, THE MODELS MOVE SO QUICKLY. HOW DO YOU SUGGEST I ELIMINATE THIS PROBLEM NEXT TIME, BEARING IN MIND THAT I'M NOT ALWAYS GIVEN A SEATED POSITION?

The show notes produced by labels/designers often note the type of fabrics used, so make sure you grab one. Then there are so many fashion blogs dedicated to analysing every last look, you might well find help online. Increasingly, shows are also being streamed online so you can watch them again and again and capture all the detail that way.

KATE CARTER

Speak to the PRs and get a rundown of the fabrics for each look. Or ask for an appointment to see the collection up close in the showroom — if you're lucky they'll say yes! *Drapers* writes the best catwalk reports for this kind of thing so buy it every Tuesday near the show season.

LUCY WOOD

CAN I GO INTO A CAREER IN FASHION JOURNALISM WITHOUT A DEGREE?

Technically, yes, but in reality I think that most employers do look for a degree as a sign of commitment, ability to work hard, meet deadlines and so on. Also, many degrees, even if not directly related to journalism, can help you learn crucial skills like how to write fast and fluently. They don't need to be journalism degrees — I studied history — but the skills are transferable.

KATE CARTER

Image: c/o *Guardian*

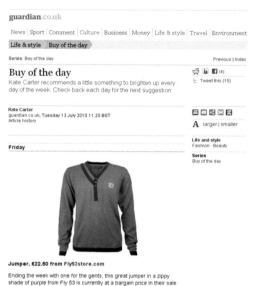

Jumper, £22.50 from Fly53store.com

Ending the week with one for the gents, this great jumper in a zippy shade of purple from Fly 53 is currently at a bargain price in their sale. Great neck detail and a lovely lightweight knit for cooler summer evenings or the approaching-too-fast autumn.

WHAT ARE THE BEST SUBJECTS TO TAKE AT HIGH SCHOOL IN ORDER TO PREPARE FOR A CAREER IN FASHION JOURNALISM?

Honestly, I think you should do whatever interests you and whatever you like the most. Obviously if you want to write for a living, a degree that involves developing these skills — whatever the subject — would be a good thing.

KATE CARTER

WHAT ARE THE DIFFERENCES BETWEEN WORKING ON FASHION PAGES FOR A MAGAZINE, NEWSPAPER AND ONLINE?

With working online the biggest difference is the timeframe. Working for a weekly or monthly magazine you have a weekly/monthly cycle of deadlines, whereas online it's constant and you try and get news stories out there as soon as possible to beat the competition, while still of course planning ahead for big events. You are also more aware of feedback, I think — your work is frequently open to comments, and you engage more directly with your readers.

KATE CARTER

On a magazine you have a little more time to plan and prepare pages, while on a newspaper the news desk can request 300 words on clogs, for instance,

and need it in 10 minutes' time – it's extremely fast-paced.
LUCY WOOD

WHAT ARE THE PERKS OF WORKING IN FASHION JOURNALISM?

Getting to see all the clothes before they hit the shops, free clothes, discount cards and fab parties!
LUCY WOOD

IS HAVING A BLOG STILL A GOOD WAY TO BECOME RECOGNISED IN THIS INDUSTRY, OR DO YOU THINK THERE ARE JUST TOO MANY FASHION BLOGS THESE DAYS?

There are a lot out there so, if you find something that no one else is doing and do it well, then yes, a fashion blog is enough to gain a presence in the industry. My advice? Have it as an extra – I love being a fashion editor on a magazine, but it's also good to be completely indulgent and feature all my favourite things on my own blog.
LUCY WOOD

Having a blog is a great thing – it gives you the ability to showcase your work and show how interested and engaged you are in the subject. But there are millions out there, so don't think of it as a reliable route to becoming recognised. Fashion

still has quite a long way to go when it comes to the internet– a lot of companies still revere magazines and they still really rule the roost.
KATE CARTER

TELL US A SECRET ABOUT WORKING IN FASHION JOURNALISM – WHAT DOES NO ONE TELL YOU BEFORE YOU START OUT?

Lots of companies will give you a press discount, which is great. Very bad for your shopping habits though!
KATE CARTER

The fashion cupboard at work becomes your wardrobe!
LUCY WOOD

CAN YOU RECOMMEND ANY INSPIRATIONAL OR INFORMATIVE WEBSITES RELATING TO FASHION JOURNALISM?

I'm obsessed with **www.fashiontoast.com** from a purely styling perspective. And **www.fashioneditoratlarge.blogspot.com** is a fashion expert's eye on things, very 'insider'. I've also been following **www.whowhatweardaily.com** for years – they're always coming up with new trends.
LUCY WOOD

Mehmet Dilsiz/Shutterstock Images LLC

To Do List

▶ **GET WRITING!** You might love the idea of being a fashion journalist and all that the role entails, but can you actually write? Now's the time to get started – put pen to paper (or fingers to keyboard), decide on a theme or story, and set yourself a deadline to produce your article. Real journalists work to tight deadlines, so it's no use giving yourself weeks to do a thousand words. Get into the habit of working quickly and with focus, and practise as much as you can. The more you practise, the easier it will be to establish where your talent lies and what sort of 'voice' or writing style you have. This will come in useful later on, when deciding which publications would suit you when doing work experience.

▶ **CREATE** your own blog. As Lucy and Kate have mentioned throughout this chapter, a blog can be a useful way to promote your work and get it seen by lots of different people. However, as they note, this is not always a fast track to success, but it's a useful tool to be able to show others your work quickly and easily, and gets you into the habit of writing on a regular basis.

▶ **START** writing articles for your school, college or university magazine or paper. This is an excellent way of producing regular work and, as you'll be writing for your fellow students, you will hear about the stories you know will interest them and have the opportunity to generate feedback on your work. If your school or college doesn't already have a publication, why not investigate ways of beginning your own? You'll also learn valuable skills in editing and managing a small team by going down this route.

▶ **GAIN** as much work experience as possible. When sending out your CV to publications, you will need to show evidence of your writing skills. Anyone can send a CV, but it will impress prospective employers if you also send a mock article you've done in the style of the magazine or newspaper you're applying to. Make sure you've done your research – know who their reader is, what appeals to them, what the writing style of the publication is – and create an article you think will suit them. You're much more likely to get called in for an interview if you've gone that extra mile to stand out from the crowd.

Don't worry if you don't live in London – not everyone will get the opportunity to work on a glossy magazine or well-known national newspaper. However, every town and city has a local newspaper and often a local magazine too, and these are great places to approach for some experience.

Exciting new hair & makeup courses and workshops!

Our Professional School is run by **Dani Guinsberg**, **Jonathan Long**, **Ben Cooke** & **Jennie Roberts**; highly experienced, well-known Fashion+Beauty Makeup Artists & Hairstylists. We offer a wide variety of specialist hair & makeup courses; suitable for anyone interested in training as a Professional Hairstylist or Makeup Artist.

Our courses are designed for beginners or Professionals wishing to increase or refresh their skills.

For more info visit:
www.thesessionschool.com
or call:
020 7224 3127

thesessionschool

IN THIS CHAPTER:

"First and foremost you must have a passion for it and be prepared to work hard."

Kate Johns, Make-up Artist

[Top to bottom] MUA: Claire Salter / Photographer: Robert Harper, MUA: Kate Johns / Photographer: Tobias Key

JOB PROFILE: MAKE-UP ARTIST

WHAT DOES A MAKE-UP ARTIST DO?

Make-up artists (MUAs) are ultimately hired for their skills in making people look as good as possible or dramatically changing how a person looks. They should have a diverse set of skills and the ability to work on many different styles of make-up, from natural to bold, high-fashion looks. MUAs will also be expected to have an understanding of hair styling, of how lighting works on a photographic fashion shoot, and of specialist skills such as cosmetic air brushing, Asian wedding make-up and body painting.

WHO EMPLOYS MAKE-UP ARTISTS?

The majority of MUAs are self-employed and work on a freelance basis. Their clients might include magazines and newspapers (editorial work), fashion companies and designers (for catwalk shows, special events and commercial work for adverts) and private clients (either for celebrities, or for customers requiring assistance with occasions such as parties or weddings). MUAs may also work on TV programmes, films and theatre productions. A select number of MUAs are employed by major cosmetics companies such as MAC to work on high-profile events and catwalk shows.

At a more commercial level, many MUAs work on the shop floor within a cosmetics store such as MAC,

MUA: Claire Salter / Photographer: Robert Harper

Space NK and Sephora, and on beauty counters within department stores. Other work can be found within spas and beauty salons.

KEY WORKING RELATIONSHIPS

As well as working directly on their model, the MUA works closely with a team of other fashion professionals. Depending on the type of job, this could include a hair stylist, photographer, fashion designer/creative or art director, and fashion stylist.

RELATED ROLES

A MUA often has other skills related to creating beauty looks/pampering, such as in hair styling, nail art, massage and facial skin therapy.

WORKING HOURS

In this sector the working hours can be very long and unconventional – this is definitely not a 9 to 5 job. MUAs have to be very flexible in order to work whenever the opportunity arises, which might mean getting up at 3am to travel to a location, waiting for hours to prepare models at a catwalk show, or spending a couple of days on location for overseas jobs. MUAs will very often work weekends, nights and over holidays.

SALARY

It can take up to a year of working for free on test shoots to build up a portfolio, then gradually you can expect approximately £50 – £100 a day, going up to £250+ a day depending on experience. A few top MUAs may earn considerably more if they are associated with a cosmetics company, have their own brand, or appear regularly on a TV programme/ have a slot in a magazine. However, for the majority of MUAs it can be hard work to earn a decent salary for the first couple of years.

EDUCATION:

There are many short courses and workshops available for beginners, as well as more in-depth programmes. Here are a few of the specialist options:

- London College of Fashion: Hair & Make-up for Fashion (Foundation Degree). LCF also runs a three-day make-up workshop for 16–18 year-olds, plus various short courses
- Session School, London: Various short courses
- The London Make-up School: various short courses
- New College, Nottingham: Make-up (NVQ full or part-time). This college also offers a 10-week Hair & Beauty Junior Academy for students 14–16 years-old
- The Cheshire Make-up Academy: various short courses

BEST THINGS ABOUT THE JOB

- Having a creative outlet and getting to do something fulfilling
- Pushing the creative limits on every assignment
- Learning something new each day

WORST THINGS ABOUT THE JOB

- Dragging heavy kit bags of make-up around when travelling to jobs
- Freelance make-up artist work is often sporadic which means some weeks can be very busy and others can be very quiet
- Jobs being postponed
- Waiting for payment for jobs

WHAT SKILLS ARE NEEDED TO BE A MAKE-UP ARTIST?

- You must show excellent attention to detail
- Be innovative – try out new things that haven't been done before
- Ability to research and get inspired by many different things, not just fashion
- Being a strong team player – make-up is a small piece of the entire puzzle and MUAs have to collaborate with many different people on a team
- Great communication skills – you must be able to communicate your ideas effectively
- Basic Photoshop skills can come in useful

(Left to right) MUA: Claire Salter / Photographer: Sarah Jones, MUA: Tomara Watkins / Photographer: Jamie Nelson

INTERVIEW: CLAIRE SALTER, MAKE-UP ARTIST

Claire Salter is a freelance make-up artist based in Nottingham. She works on lots of interesting jobs, from editorial, fashion shows and advertising to music videos and TV. Claire's client base has included Adidas, Boo Hoo, Urban Outfitters, Ben Sherman, John Smedley, GHD, Boots and many more. Her work can be seen at: www.clairesalter.co.uk

WHICH SUBJECTS DID YOU STUDY AT HIGH SCHOOL?
Art & Design, Textiles, Home Economics, Maths, Social Science, Biology, English Language & Literature.

WHICH COLLEGE DID YOU GO TO? I studied fashion design at West Notts College. In later life I went back to college to study the Pathways course in make-up artistry at NCN (New College Nottingham) and was taught by an amazing lecturer called April Green.

WHAT MADE YOU GET INTO MAKE-UP? I've always experimented with my own hair and make-up (and made some crazy fashion statements). But it wasn't until I had a very unfortunate year I thought to myself, 'What am I doing with my life?' I knew I needed a new direction but had no idea what to do. I was in a restaurant where the waitress mentioned she was moving to London to do make-up artistry. It was as if someone had hit me with a magic wand and that was when I decided to go back to college to study make-up. I've never looked back.

WHAT'S THE MOST DRAMATIC MAKE-UP YOU'VE EVER DONE? I think this is best said in pictures. It's not just about proving how creative you are. When I started out I used glitter, gold leaf, feathers, all kinds of crazy stuff but it's about striking a balance. I think the shot on the right shows creativity yet restraint.

DO YOU CONSIDER DOING MAKE-UP AS A KIND OF ART?
Yes! I love creating a look and then seeing it all come to life on the shoot when the model feels the mood and the photographer feels it too.

HOW MUCH DID YOU GET PAID WHEN YOU STARTED OUT? Nothing! When you start out you're expected to work/test for free. I tested for two years before I felt confident enough to show the world my portfolio.

I'm very fortunate I have a very understanding mum, Linda Salter, who has supported me along the way.

WHO IS THE MOST FAMOUS PERSON YOU'VE MADE UP, AND WHAT WAS THE EXPERIENCE LIKE? One that sticks in my mind is Amber Le Bon. We were shooting swimwear on a rainy day in South London and the shoot took place in a disused car park. We didn't exactly break in, there was already a hole in the fence so we climbed through, set up and began to shoot. After a short while a security van came hurtling down the road, yellow lights flashing. We were asked to leave so we tried to talk our way out of it and told them we were students shooting our final collection. The security guy was having none of it so we packed up all our kit and moved on. We ended up shooting on the streets and in a petrol station. Amber was a pleasure to work with – she never moaned, or got stroppy, she just got on with the job.

WHAT HAS BEEN YOUR LEAST FAVOURITE MAKE-UP JOB AND WHY? It was for a model's portfolio. All I can say is that I had to do a lot of repair work! Considering she wanted to break into the industry, she was very ungroomed. I had to patch up her fake tan, pluck her facial hair, file her nails and try to disguise her dark roots. I also had to remove layers of make-up before I could even begin. To be honest there really is no bad job. Every job/test you do has something beneficial to it – even if you make a mistake, or something goes horribly wrong, it's all a learning curve and you will know next time how to approach the situation better.

WHAT IS YOUR TOP BEAUTY TIP? Create a great base to work on. I love Mac Prep and Prime, which calms, soothes and evens out skin redness. Always use a good foundation. One of my favourites is Bobbi Brown Moisture Rich, which delivers a soft, beautiful finish and is great for photo shoots. To make the model look refreshed, I like YSL Touche Eclat which is ideal for banishing under-eye shadows. I place the product on the back of my hand first and then use a small concealer brush to apply it. Once you've mastered a great base, the fun begins...

Smiley Claire

MUA: Claire Salter / Photographer: James Lightbown

Tomara Watkins: With five years of experience, Tomara is a freelance make-up artist based in New York. She does editorial, shows and some advertising work. You can see her work at: **www.twatkinsbeauty.com**

Kate Johns: Kate trained in 2005 and has been working on a freelance basis since then. The majority of her work is fashion and editorial, photo shoot and show based.
See her work at: www.katejohns.com

Claire Salter: Read more about Claire on the previous page.

WHAT IS YOUR FAVOURITE TYPE OF WORK?

I love working on editorials. My favourite and most interesting was working on a body-painting assignment. It was a long shoot with five different looks, but it was inspiring.
TOMARA WATKINS

WHAT INTERESTING JOBS HAVE YOU WORKED ON?

I have recently worked on a shoot for Browns. It featured some fantastic one-off pieces by designers such as Balenciaga, Stella McCartney and Missoni that had been created to celebrate the shops' 40th birthday. Another interesting job I collaborated

MUA: Claire Salter / Photographer: Robert Harper

on was a shoot for *Idol* magazine which included amazing clothes and was a chance to create some really vibrant make-up looks.
KATE JOHNS

WHAT DOES AN AVERAGE DAY INVOLVE?

Generally there is no average day, as all jobs are different. On a photo shoot the day starts with the hair stylist creating the model's hair and then I will do their make-up. I have to be on set all day to make sure the make-up looks flawless in the photos, so I have to be on hand for touch-ups and any look changes that are required. This is not a 9 to 5 career. There is no average length of a working day.
KATE JOHNS

DO YOU DRAW OUT THE LAYOUT OF YOUR IDEAS ON PAPER BEFORE APPLYING THE MAKE-UP TO THE MODEL?

Yes and no. Sometimes, if I'm not sure where I want to go with something, I do face charts. If I am sure what direction I want to go in I just print out reference photographs.
TOMARA WATKINS

HOW DO YOU DECIDE ON THE LOOK OR THEME FOR A JOB?

Generally the look for a job is a result of collaboration between the photographer, stylist, hairstylist and myself.
KATE JOHNS

HOW DO YOU GO ABOUT FINDING NEW JOBS?

It is a constant hustle. You have to network with everyone — art directors, editors, creative directors and photographers — anyone that is part of the creative team. Sometimes a wardrobe stylist or hair stylist can recommend you for a job. Marketing is key! It doesn't matter how good you are if no one knows about it.
TOMARA WATKINS

WHAT SHOULD A WANNABE MAKE-UP ARTIST HAVE IN THEIR PORTFOLIO?

You need to showcase your talent. I think that sometimes, when starting out, make-up artists feel that in order to be seen as talented they have to create lots of outlandish looks and of course this shows your creativity, but you should also bear in mind that you must be able to show that you can create clean and flawless beauty looks. There are not many clients that call for the ability to stick feathers and jewels to a model's face! I feel it is important to show your diversity, so make sure you show that you can create any look that is asked for.
KATE JOHNS

WHAT ARE YOUR ESSENTIAL TOOLS WHEN WORKING ON A JOB?

A magnifying glass (don't rely on retouching) to see how the skin will look on film/digital, water, sponges, palettes (you want to try to condense as much as possible), mascara — and a great attitude.
TOMARA WATKINS

TELL US A SECRET ABOUT WORKING IN THIS SECTOR (THAT NO ONE EVER MENTIONS BEFORE YOU START OUT)

Your skill means nothing if no one knows about it. You really have to market yourself and network to get jobs. There is a fine line between art and commerce in this business and that is the side that make-up artists seem to struggle with.
TOMARA WATKINS

WHAT IS YOUR TOP BEAUTY TIP?

Good skin is the foundation of make-up. Without the proper skincare products, make-up doesn't look its best.
TOMARA WATKINS

Never go to bed without taking off your make-up. Ever!
KATE JOHNS

DID YOU HAVE TO WORK FOR FREE WHEN YOU STARTED OUT?

Absolutely! I didn't mind, because I was learning so much about the business. If a project is worth it to me now, I would still work for free...
TOMARA WATKINS

Yes. When building your portfolio most make-up artists will work on a TFP (test for portfolio) basis, which means that all involved are working for payment in images.
KATE JOHNS

IN YOUR OPINION IS IT ESSENTIAL TO HAVE QUALIFICATIONS TO WORK IN MAKE-UP?

Not at all. I never went to a make-up school. I went to the real school of beauty — the make-up counter and my friends.
TOMARA WATKINS

I know make-up artists who have paid a lot of money for a course; I also know make-up artists who are self-trained. Since completing my course I have never been asked for my qualifications. Your work is judged on the shots in your portfolio — this includes the quality of the model, styling, hair and photography.
CLAIRE SALTER

I don't think it's imperative but it helps. I learnt a lot from my make-up education and I'm glad that I took a course. The majority of people that I work with have qualifications in the field.
KATE JOHNS

MUA: Tomara Watkins / Photographer: Melissa Scheetz

WHERE DID YOU TRAIN?

I went to the Glauca Rossi School of make-up in London. I thought it was great. There are so many courses out there, and new make-up schools and courses seem to be starting up all the time. I would advise anyone wanting to take a course to visit a few. Also it depends on what type of make-up you're interested in as often schools specialise in certain disciplines such as make-up for television and special effects.
KATE JOHNS

I'M STILL AT SCHOOL/COLLEGE – WHAT CAN I DO NOW TO BEGIN PREPARING FOR A CAREER IN MAKE-UP?

I consider working on a make-up counter the real school of beauty. You encounter women with all different types of skin tone, eye shape, etc. That is the best place to learn and you can also start to build a good kit by buying products with staff discount.
TOMARA WATKINS

Contact working make-up artists and offer your assistance. You may only be making the tea, or washing their brushes, but this will open you up to how the industry works and what is expected of you on a shoot. You may also get a credit in a magazine tear sheet. This will then enable you to contact more make-up artists in the hope of assisting them.
CLAIRE SALTER

MUA: Claire Salter / Photographer: Gary Steer

HOW SHOULD I GO ABOUT GETTING WORK EXPERIENCE ASSISTING A MAKE-UP ARTIST?

Contact agencies that represent make-up artists and let them know you are interested. You must have a portfolio when contacting agencies, unless you know the artist personally.
TOMARA WATKINS

Do your research, contact the MUA or their agent, always personalise your e-mail, check out their website and comment on their work. Never text, as this can come across as bad manners. Keep your e-mail brief and add some examples of your work, plus all your contact details. Be willing, eager and polite.
CLAIRE SALTER

WILL MAKE-UP ARTISTS TAKE PEOPLE ON FOR WORK EXPERIENCE WHO ARE STILL AT HIGH SCHOOL?

I would, but it depends on the artist. I wish someone had been available for me at that age. As a high-school student, if you show thirst for the career I am sure an artist would take you just as seriously as someone who is older.
TOMARA WATKINS

WHAT ARE YOUR TOP TIPS FOR THOSE LOOKING TO GET INTO MAKE-UP ARTISTRY?

First and foremost you must have a passion for it and be prepared to work hard.
KATE JOHNS

Be prepared to make sacrifices, to travel, work long hours and work for free. Don't expect to get rich quick. Keep your kit clean at all times.
CLAIRE SALTER

I'VE HEARD THAT SOME MAKE-UP SCHOOLS OFFER TRAINING COURSES THAT ONLY LAST A FEW WEEKS. IS THAT LONG ENOUGH TO LEARN THE BASICS OR SHOULD I TAKE A COURSE THAT'S AT LEAST A YEAR?

The course I took was a year long and included all aspects of the industry, from skin care, creating a natural look, high fashion, theatrical, basic special FX, styling, colour analysis, nails, hair and photo shoots.

I think you could learn the basics on a shorter course, but you don't really start to learn the industry and what is expected of you until you complete your course and get out there testing.
CLAIRE SALTER

To Do List

▶ **PRACTISE** creating different make-up looks on models. If you aren't yet at college or uni, use your family and friends to test your skills on. If you're already on a fashion — or beauty-related course you should have no problem finding suitable models who are willing to assist — most other students will also be needing to create test shots for their portfolios. If you're looking to get on to a make-up course or get work experience within this sector, you will almost certainly have to provide evidence of your skills by showing images of work in a portfolio. Try to present a diverse range of looks — some dramatic, some natural make-up and some examples of more artistic/fantasy looks.

▶ **RESEARCH** the work of other make-up artists online and by reading specialist books on the subject. Two great books to look out for are *Making Faces* by Kevyn Aucoin and *Makeup Your Mind* by Francois Nars. These are great sources of inspiration and are also good for learning more about specific techniques. You can see online portfolios on websites such as **www.iqons.com**, **www.nineteen74. com**, **www.whoistesting.com** and **www.modelmayhem.com**. You should also look on blogs and YouTube for practical tips on make-up application, such as the one by Lauren Luke: **www.laurenluke.co.uk**

▶ **FIND** some work experience. As mentioned earlier in this chapter, work experience is the best way of learning on the job and making contacts. Don't worry if you aren't based in a major city — make-up artists are based in many different locations, not just in London, Paris, Milan and New York. Search online for MUAs in your area — most artists are freelance, so will have their own web page or blog, making it easy to contact them direct. You should also offer assistance working on school/college fashion shows or theatre productions and also on local charity fashion shows, where you might be able to help out backstage. Also research a few beauty salons in your area to see if you can assist a MUA there.

Register to win an SC51 shirt
www.SC51.co.uk

IN THIS CHAPTER:

"I wasn't aware that the role would involve working with so many celebrities, which of course is a great perk."

Emily-Kate Pawley, Marketing Assistant

Image: Katsiaryna/Shutterstock Images

WHAT DOES A PR/MARKETING PERSON DO?

The PR (public relations) and marketing departments work alongside each other, and their role is primarily to promote the products/services of the company they work for in the best possible manner to the general public and their consumers. They do this by overseeing media campaigns, arranging product launches and organising parties and fashion shows. PR and marketing campaigns are conducted using the traditional press and media (magazines, newspapers, radio and TV) and increasingly through websites, blogs and social networks such as Twitter, Facebook and YouTube.

A PR person's role is focused on optimising good news about their company or brand, and down-playing bad news, meaning they are often dealing with the unexpected. A marketing person is more involved with developing longer-term strategies, making sure the '7 Ps' are presented in the correct way to their customers. These are: product, price, promotion, place, people, process and physical evidence.

WHO EMPLOYS FASHION PR/MARKETING PROFESSIONALS?

Opportunities exist to work in all types of company, including independent designers, retailers, brands and luxury companies, and in event management, magazines and forecasting agencies. PR and marketing professionals either work for agencies (which represent several companies, designers and brands, so the employee would juggle the work of several different clients) or in-house with a company (where they would work solely on the products and brands of that company) and there's a pretty even split between working full-time or freelance.

KEY WORKING RELATIONSHIPS

In a major fashion company, the team is usually overseen by a marketing or PR director with several managers reporting to them. The managers then look after any marketing/PR assistants and interns. Some fashion companies have large PR/marketing departments, while some just have one marketing person and one PR person who co-ordinates everything (or sometimes one person might do both PR and marketing). They will liaise with their creative/design director, buying teams (if working in a retail brand), graphic designers and visual teams. In addition to their immediate colleagues, PR and marketing professionals will be in contact with many other people on a daily basis, including consumers, retailers, designers, stylists, creative/advertising agencies, journalists, sales people and celebrity/model agencies.

RELATED ROLES

It's relatively easy for someone who has worked in marketing to transfer into PR, and vice-versa. Opportunities also exist for PR/marketing professionals to go into journalism, teaching, advertising, forecasting and event management, because of the flexible nature of their skills and wealth of industry contacts.

WORKING HOURS

Officially these tend to be 8.30am to 6pm, but most employees work much longer because these roles are focused towards social/networking events. They are expected to promote their company at every opportunity, and this includes late nights, lunch times and weekends, going to parties, store openings, product launches, fashion shows and meetings with clients and journalists.

SALARY

A graduate could hope to start at about £16k, with pay rising as their experience grows. For a London-based head of marketing, salary can be anywhere from £40k to £100k, depending on the size of the company.

EDUCATION:

While it's possible to work your way up by doing work experience within an agency or brand, this sector is a very popular choice and extremely competitive, so it will give your CV a boost if you can gain specialist qualifications. Here are a few suitable courses (most fashion marketing and management courses will also cover modules on PR):

- Northumbria University: BA (Hons) Fashion Marketing
- UCA Epsom: BA (Hons) Fashion Management & Marketing
- University of Northampton: BA (Hons) Fashion Marketing

BEST THINGS ABOUT THE JOB

- Working with designers and other creative people every day and being involved in lots of different projects that are all happening at the same time
- Being able to communicate your ideas to the public
- Meeting influential people within the industry

WORST THINGS ABOUT THE JOB

- Sometimes you have to work long hours to get a project finished on time but that is all part of the job
- There are the mundane things such as administrative tasks, but most office-based roles will involve tasks like this

WHAT SKILLS ARE NEEDED TO WORK IN FASHION PR/MARKETING?

- Excellent writing skills
- You need to be confident, patient, persuasive and a great communicator – good people skills are a must, as this is a very social job
- You should be super-organised and able to work to (and meet) deadlines
- Ability to manage a budget carefully and allocate funds to the right projects
- You must be able to spot consumer trends quickly and react to them if they are relevant to your brand
- Good IT skills
- Excellent telephone manner

Image courtesy of Haymarket Exhibitions

Arieta is based in London and is PR Manager for River Island, where she oversees the day-to-day running of the press office as well as being responsible for overall PR strategy. She's been working in PR for eight years and has also worked for New Look.

EDUCATION
GCSEs: Maths, English, Science, History, Art
A-levels: IT, Law, Sociology and Media Studies
University: Arieta completed an HND in Business & Marketing at London Metropolitan University, then did a degree in Business Law at Brighton University

Industry Insider

DID YOU GO INTO PR IMMEDIATELY AFTER GRADUATION? IF NOT, WHAT DID YOU DO? No, I didn't go into PR straight away — I worked as a visual merchandiser and as a window display dresser while also doing an internship at *Smash Hits* magazine.

WHAT MADE YOU GET INTO PR? I love meeting people and I love fashion, and working in fashion PR has given me the opportunity to do both.

DID YOU DO WORK EXPERIENCE EARLY IN YOUR CAREER? Yes, indeed, after *Smash Hits* I went on to *Sneak* magazine then interned at New Look before I got the job as a press assistant there.

WHAT'S BEEN THE MOST EXCITING PROJECT YOU'VE WORKED ON, AND WHY? Getting both Kelis and Ashley Banjo as the 'faces' of Graduate Fashion Week (when River Island were the main sponsor of the event). I oversaw all negotiations, then got to style, organise and direct the shoot all by myself. My bosses liked the end result and that felt really good.

WHAT'S BEEN THE MOST CHALLENGING PROJECT YOU'VE WORKED ON AND WHY? Every day is a challenge in PR as today you may be 'in' and tomorrow you may not. We also have to deal with some very tricky celebrities and it's sometimes hard keeping the right balance and making sure everyone is happy.

IS WORKING IN PR CREATIVE OR NOT? HOW MUCH FREEDOM DO YOU GET WHEN PLANNING PROJECTS? Working in PR is very creative and you do get some freedom, but you need to remember that every project needs to be 'on brand' (in line with the core brand identity) and as a result the director of fashion communications will make the ultimate decisions and have the final say in what happens.

HOW MUCH TRAVEL DO YOU DO IN YOUR JOB, AND WHERE DO YOU GET TO GO? As PR Manager I get to travel once in a while throughout the UK and sometimes internationally.

> "One of the most exciting projects I've worked on included securing both Kelis and Ashley Banjo as the 'faces' of Graduate Fashion Week."

Arieta looking fierce!

Photo of Arieta Mujay: Dennis Lye

Emily-Kate Pawley is a Marketing Assistant for the London-based media and events company Haymarket Exhibitions, where she's been working as an intern for a year since graduating from university. She is responsible for helping with high-profile events such as Clothes Show Live and Clothes Show London, where she is involved in the organisation and marketing of the exhibitions, seminars and catwalk shows.

EDUCATION
GCSEs: English, English Lit, Maths, Science, Textiles, Drama, Geography, German
A-levels: Art (fashion/textiles), Geography, Photography, Performing Arts
University: BA (Hons) Fashion Media & Promotion at Northbrook College, Sussex

Industry Insider

WHERE DID YOU WORK BEFORE THE CLOTHES SHOW?
When I was at university, I had a number of part-time jobs including working in bars and a nightclub in my first year and then in my second and third year I worked part time for Oasis.

DID YOU GO INTO MARKETING IMMEDIATELY AFTER GRADUATION? Kind of – I got an internship with Haymarket Exhibitions. I started out as an operations assistant, working on a number of different shows including Clothes Show Live, Masterchef Live and the BBC Good Food Show. I was in this job role for six months before moving on to marketing assistant for the Clothes Show marketing team.

WHAT MADE YOU DECIDE TO GO INTO MARKETING?
It's an area of the fashion industry that I have always been interested in and then when I went to university we had a number of marketing projects throughout the three years of my course. I found it really interesting and looked forward to the marketing lectures more than the design ones. That made me realise that this was the area of the fashion industry that I wanted to focus on.

DID YOU DO WORK EXPERIENCE WHILE YOU WERE AT UNI? During my second year at university I had the opportunity to take part in a four-month work placement at Graduate Fashion Week. I worked at the head office, assisting the event director to ensure that the event ran smoothly.

HOW DID YOU GET YOUR CURRENT ROLE – WHAT WAS YOUR ROUTE IN? My former manager at Graduate Fashion Week put me in touch with the company that I work for now. I sent off my CV and cover letter to the Managing Director, who then got in touch about the one-year internship that I am currently doing – and I've never looked back!

WHAT DOES YOUR CURRENT ROLE INVOLVE? There are many responsibilities that I have to cover on a daily basis, such as handling exhibitor and visitor enquires, making sure that the social sites that we use (Facebook, Twitter, MySpace) are updated each day and are interactive for our friends and followers. I also assist the Marketing Executive on website design and content, which involves writing the copy for the website and making sure it's frequently updated, and I write copy for our newsletter e-mails which go out regularly to our visitor database. While on site at the Clothes Show I've been responsible for looking after features such as the Celebrity Santa's Grotto and Stop & Chop.

WHAT'S BEEN THE MOST EXCITING PROJECT YOU'VE WORKED ON, AND WHY? The most exciting project I've worked on during this job is the Celebrity Santa's Grotto. I loved it because it was my own little area to manage in the show. I had to ensure that the feature ran smoothly and on time, by making sure that the crowd was under control and that the celebrities were being looked after well and that they were prepared and punctual for the event.

IS WORKING IN MARKETING AS YOU EXPECTED IT TO BE?
It is exactly as I thought it would be and with extra perks! While at uni, we covered all the basics in marketing, so I was aware of the type of things that would need to be done. However, I wasn't aware that the role would entail working with so many celebrities, which of course is a fabulous perk.

Emily-Kate

Images courtesy of Haymarket Exhibitions

Our expert panel includes Arieta Mujay, PR Manager for River Island, and Emily-Kate Pawley from Haymarket (read more about Arieta and Emily on the previous pages), together with Jo Eaton from SC51. Together they tackle your questions on getting into fashion PR & marketing.

Jo Eaton: With 12 years of industry experience, Jo is Marketing Manager for SC51. She previously worked with the menswear brand Sonneti for six years in the capacity of Marketing Manager and prior to this she worked in fashion recruitment with two leading London-based talent agencies. She holds a BA (Hons) in Fashion Marketing from Northumbria University.

WHAT DOES AN AVERAGE DAY INVOLVE?

Every day is different but some of the general tasks include liaising with the fashion and consumer press to get publicity for the brand, planning special projects to promote the brand (for example, with bands and celebrities), managing the Facebook and Twitter accounts, writing blogs, organising photo shoots, talking to customers... the list goes on!
JO EATON

Going through the magazines and the daily papers to identify coverage, ringing around the fashion publications to find out what stories they might be working on, and ensuring samples get sent out. We also liaise with celebrity agents to get their clients dressed in River Island, and are in constant contact with our buying team to ensure we have the right samples in.
ARIETA MUJAY

WHAT ARE THE PERKS OF WORKING IN MARKETING?

You get to be out and about a lot and it can be a very social job with parties and fashion shows to attend. You get to meet lots of cool people and can sometimes get free clothes (I work on menswear brands so the men I know are very happy!).
JO EATON

You go to some really awesome parties and get to know key fashion trends a season in advance.
ARIETA MUJAY

WHAT SHOULD A WANNABE FASHION MARKETING/PR ASSISTANT TAKE ALONG TO AN INTERVIEW?

Just yourself and your CV. Although in your head you must have lots of research about the brand and its competitors. It's great to have ideas and suggestions for the brand but as long as you have done your research you should go a long way.
JO EATON

WHAT ARE THE AVERAGE WORKING HOURS IN FASHION PR/MARKETING?

Every day and every hour can be work – at weekends you should always be looking out for potential opportunities for your brand and always have the brand at the back of your mind. It's very common to stay late to finish projects, or take work home with you.
JO EATON

HOW MUCH CROSS-OVER IS THERE BETWEEN MARKETING AND PR – ARE THE ROLES VERY SIMILAR?

The roles do cross over, although PR can tend to be more creative and marketing more strategic.
JO EATON

Marketing and PR go hand in hand. You cannot successfully execute a PR strategy without marketing, and vice versa.
ARIETA MUJAY

HOW MUCH TRAVEL DO YOU DO IN YOUR JOB, AND WHERE DO YOU GET TO GO?

The amount of travel depends on the size of the brand you are working for and the budgets they have available. You might get to visit a glamorous location to direct a photo shoot or you might go to trade shows across Europe or the rest of the world. On the other hand, you may just visit your retailers around the country. Whatever the budget, you are not tied to your desk every day, there is plenty to do.
JO EATON

TELL US A SECRET ABOUT WORKING IN FASHION PR/MARKETING

There are lots of opinionated people in the fashion industry and you can't please all of the people all of the time!
JO EATON

Image courtesy of Haymarket Exhibitions

It's hard work and you don't get paid much when starting out. A lot of people who start out in fashion don't make it as they don't anticipate the amount of work that needs to be done for such little pay.
ARIETA MUJAY

IN YOUR OPINION DO PEOPLE HAVE TO HAVE A DEGREE TO WORK IN FASHION PR/MARKETING?

No, not really. It can help if you have one, but this business is all about networking and getting contacts as well as knowing and keeping up to date with the trends.
ARIETA MUJAY

It is ideal to have a degree to get your foot in the door of the fashion industry, as there is so much competition out there. Plus it gives you time to gain more contacts and work experience while you are studying.
JO EATON

WHAT ARE YOUR TOP TIPS FOR THOSE LOOKING TO GET INTO FASHION PR/MARKETING?

Use all the contacts you have and, if you don't have any, get some! Make sure you are up to date with all areas of current affairs and social trends and get some retail work experience. This helps you to see how marketing is used in store and how it can affect a brand's credibility.
JO EATON

Get loads of work experience under your belt, as in PR the old saying is true: It's not what you know, it's who you know. Study and get very familiar with fashion magazines, e.g. *Vogue*, *Bazaar*, *Elle*, etc. You also need to know what the key fashion websites are and be able to navigate your way through them.
ARIETA MUJAY

IS THIS JOB EXTREMELY COMPETITIVE TO GET INTO?

Yes, very. There are a lot of people who don't want to go into fashion design, and PR/marketing is often their first option.
JO EATON

HOW CAN I MAKE MYSELF STAND OUT WHEN APPLYING FOR WORK EXPERIENCE?

Make sure your cover letter and CV are short and sweet. Don't ramble on. Make them look attractive but don't overdo it on the design front — you want to get your CV noticed, but it needs to be clear enough

for the recipient to want to read on.
EMILY-KATE PAWLEY

Research, research, research — and an easy-to-understand CV, with relevant experience!
JO EATON

Be interesting and be truthful. If you lie on your CV, it only takes a phone call to verify the information, so you would be found out easily.
ARIETA MUJAY

ARE THERE ANY OPPORTUNITIES FOR WORK EXPERIENCE IN PR/MARKETING FOR STUDENTS WHO ARE STILL AT SCHOOL?

Yes, but you must have lots of confidence to get your foot in the door. Persistence is key.
JO EATON

Yes, apply to marketing agencies, or companies that have in-house marketing departments. You will be there to assist on normal day-to-day duties — it's not all exciting tasks, and they may get you making cups of tea and stuffing envelopes. But keep your eyes and ears open, you may get stuck with the not so glamorous jobs — but watch what those are doing around you and what they are saying — you will be surprised what you pick up.
EMILY-KATE PAWLEY

ARE THERE ANY WEBSITES YOU WOULD RECOMMEND RELATED TO FASHION PR/MARKETING?

The internet is full of good advice to build up your knowledge of the industry. Look at brands' and retailers' sites, fashion marketing recruitment websites and use YouTube and fashion/social networking sites to make contacts.
JO EATON

www.fashionmonitor.com / www.diarydirectory.com / www.WGSN.com
ARIETA MUJAY

IS WORKING IN MARKETING CREATIVE OR NOT?

Marketing can be very creative, especially when it comes to producing campaigns. Here at the Clothes Show, we come up with the ideas and then we brief a design agency to make those ideas happen. These will fly back and forth between us and the agency until we are happy with the final product.
EMILY-KATE PAWLEY

To Do List

▶ **NETWORK** As Arieta mentioned earlier in this chapter, it's not what you know, it's WHO you know. It's never too early to begin building a network of contacts. This should be by meeting people at events (parties, exhibitions, consumer and trade shows such as Graduate Fashion Week and the Clothes Show) as well as online. Get talking to people at these events — you never know who you might be hobnobbing with! Always take an interest in what people are doing and the projects they're involved with. Show confidence and be friendly — a smile goes a long way too. This sector is all about your people skills — you aren't going to get very far by being the grumpy-looking one in the corner. You can also build contacts by joining networking websites online (take a look in the Further Reading/Useful sites section at the back of this book for a list) — but make sure that your profile is written in a professional manner and is double-checked for spelling mistakes before you upload it.

▶ **GET WORK EXPERIENCE** Although it's great to get some experience within a fashion company/agency, don't worry too much if you can't get specialist fashion work. Most cities have a couple of generalist PR/Marketing agencies you could approach, where you will be able to learn the basics of the business and pick up skills such as client account management and writing press releases, You are also likely to be given general administration tasks such as meeting and greeting clients, dealing with queries on the phone and via e-mail, and also filing and photocopying. All of this will give you a basic understanding of what goes on in a busy PR/Marketing department or agency, and will provide you with great transferable skills you can use within a more specialist fashion company.

Welcome to a place that unlocks your creative potential.

www.cc-creativeworkshops.co.uk

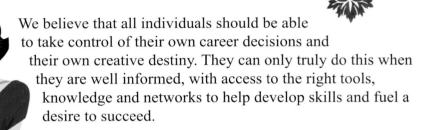

We believe that all individuals should be able to take control of their own career decisions and their own creative destiny. They can only truly do this when they are well informed, with access to the right tools, knowledge and networks to help develop skills and fuel a desire to succeed.

The CC Creative Workshops is an organisation dedicated to providing support, giving real experiences and industry led projects in schools, colleges and universities.

Programmes that inspire creativity... 'This is Creative Enterprise'

It is increasingly noticeable within the educational system today; young people are being inspired to use their creative potential and move into the professional arts and creative industries also to think out enterprise as a viable career venture.

Together the CC-Creative Workshops and the talents of the students participating introduce www.thisiscreativeenterprise.com. Here you will find a array of creative talent, student profiles and work, and all the information to get involved.

...this is
creative
enterprise...

CHAPTER EIGHT: FASHION BUYING

IN THIS CHAPTER:

"You get to indulge your passion for fashion on a daily basis and work in one of the most exciting industries in the world. You kind of get to shop for a living!"

Emma Clark, Buying Recruitment Consultant

Images: Sally McEntyre c/o Bestseller

WHAT DOES A FASHION BUYER DO?

Buyers have a lot of power in the industry, and ultimately decide what product goes into the stores. There are two different types of buyer — product development buyers and selection buyers. Selection buying is seen as the more glamorous of the two, as this role offers the opportunity to collaborate with designers and select the most exciting pieces from their collections through attending their fashion shows, going to private buying events and visiting the showrooms. In this job, you are required to be more analytical than in product development buying, and there is less creativity involved. A product development buyer works closely with the design team providing their input on how the ranges will look in store. They will follow each product throughout the whole process, from initial discussion of key trends at the beginning of the season, to establishing which pieces go into the ranges once the prototypes have arrived back from the suppliers/ factories.

It's the responsibility of the buyer to come up with a balanced and cohesive range, including deciding on what colours each piece should be, negotiating the best price to buy at from the suppliers, and then fixing a price to retail at.

The structure of a buying team depends on the size of the company. But, generally speaking, at entry level you would start off as a buyer's admin assistant (BAA), progressing to buyer's assistant (BA), then you might become a junior buyer. After a few years you would be able to call yourself a buyer, before going on to be a senior buyer, and ultimately a head of buying or buying manager. Within larger retailers, it's common for employees to work on one or two product categories. These would be clothing or accessories, which might then be further broken down — for instance, some buyers have responsibility just for men's socks or ladies' denim. In smaller retailers, the buyer is likely to work across lots of different product categories.

WHO EMPLOYS BUYERS?

Product development buyers tend to be employed by high-street retailers and department stores, from Topshop and Primark, to John Lewis and House of Fraser. Selection buyers work for independent boutiques and online retailers.

KEY WORKING RELATIONSHIPS

Buyers work very closely with the design team, merchandisers, the product development team, and their supply base either in the UK or overseas.

RELATED ROLES

Selection buyers are often able to make the transition into merchandising, as these roles overlap quite a lot. Or they might switch over to the wholesale side to work for a supplier. This involves advising the retail buyers what products to develop for their ranges, translating this information back to the factories, then putting the samples into production and negotiating prices with the factory in order to pass on to the retail buyers.

WORKING HOURS

For employees in a high-street retailer working hours are typically 8.30am to 6pm on an average day, but it's common to work at weekends and do overtime, especially when on buying trips.

SALARY

This depends on the type of company you work for and where you're located. Here is a guide to what to expect in London:

BAA: £16k—£20k
BA: £20k—£28k
Junior Buyer: £28k—£35k
Buyer: £36k—£50k
Senior Buyer: £50k—£65k
Head of Buying: £70k—£100k

Once you become more senior, you can normally expect a bonus and benefits package that might include a car allowance, private medical insurance, pension, etc.

EDUCATION:

Useful high school/sixth-form subjects: English, Maths, Science, Art & Design, IT

The majority of buyers have a degree (in fashion or another subject), but it's sometimes possible to work your way up either from a sales-related role, or from a more vocational course such as a diploma. Here are a few specialist courses to consider:

- Fashion & Retail Academy, London: Level 4 Diploma, Buying & Merchandising
- University of Huddersfield: BA (Hons) Fashion & Textile Buying
- De Montfort University, Leicester: BA (Hons) Retail Buying
- University of Westminster, London: BA Fashion Buying Management

BEST THINGS ABOUT THE JOB

For me, the best thing about working in buying is that I get to be in touch with the product that I love. Before I studied fashion, my first experience of the industry as I was growing up was my mother's love of designer accessories so this is where it all started for me. To be working surrounded by this product every day and constantly learning more about it is so exciting.
FAYE BAMBER

You get to indulge your passion for fashion on a daily basis and work in one of the most exciting industries in the world. You kind of get to shop for a living!
EMMA CLARK

WORST THINGS ABOUT THE JOB

In my role at entry level in buying, there is always a lot of work to be done that is administrative, but this is the nature of the job, especially within a branded department.
FAYE BAMBER

You have to be 100 per cent committed, as working in buying often involves very long hours and, at the beginning of your career, very little pay.
EMMA CLARK

WHAT SKILLS ARE NEEDED TO BE A FASHION BUYER?

You need to have a good eye, and be creative and passionate about fashion. Ideally, you need to be fairly good at maths and have an analytical nature, although I know plenty of buyers who can only add up with a calculator.
EMMA CLARK

Image: Sally McEntyre c/o Bestseller

Based in London, Faye is a Buyer's Assistant for ASOS, where she works on premium womenswear and branded accessories. This is her first postgraduate role in buying. Here she gives an insight into what it's like to work with one of the UK's most successful online retailers.

EDUCATION
GCSEs: English Language & Literature, Maths, Double Science, French, German, Spanish, Textile Technology, History, RE
College: Faye went to Winstanley College (Wigan) where she did AS-level Psychology, and A-levels in French, German, Textiles, Art & Design. She then went on to do a Foundation course in Art & Design
University: BA (Hons) Fashion Design and Technology — Womenswear at London College of Fashion

Industry Insider!

YOU TRAINED IN DESIGN — WHY DID YOU DECIDE TO GO DOWN THE BUYING ROUTE INSTEAD? While studying for my degree, I realised that, as much as I enjoyed it, it may not have been 100 per cent the correct role for me in the industry. Initially I decided to study design as this was the only part of fashion that was ever fully explained to me as a career path.

Once I moved to London and saw that there were many more options, I became very proactive in searching for a wide variety of work placements to aid me upon graduating. This led to me working in buying, press, wholesale sales, design and production. Of all the placements I completed I felt that I enjoyed buying the most and that it suited me the best.

WHAT PROCESS DID YOU GO THROUGH TO GET YOUR ROLE AT ASOS? The way in which I got my job at ASOS was not along the usual route. Once I graduated from university I began looking for my first job straight away but at the time there were not many jobs anywhere in the industry. So, in the meantime, I undertook another work placement in wholesale; when I was not working on my placement I was permanently looking for a job and getting back in touch with everyone I had met or worked for in the industry.

I had been lucky enough to meet someone that worked for ASOS, and through them was offered a work placement in the buying office. While there I continued to look for a permanent job until the Buyer's Assistant I was working for moved departments. I was interviewed for the job along with other candidates from inside the business (also on work placements), as well as some from outside, and was lucky enough to be offered the job.

WHAT INTERNSHIPS DID YOU DO AT UNI, AND HOW DID THEY PREPARE YOU FOR YOUR CURRENT ROLE? I completed many internships at university but the main ones were: Buyer's Intern at Selfridges, Design & Production Intern at Launer & Co., Press Intern at Moschino (which led to me working as the Press Assistant), Press Intern at Arcadia and Wholesale Intern at Moschino.

All the various internships I completed prepared me for life on leaving university, as they taught me about the fashion industry as a whole. I felt that on my course at university I only really learnt about and understood design and it seemed very unrealistic. By completing all the diverse internships that I did, I understood how each part of the industry worked together and the importance of them all as a whole rather than stand-alone jobs.

WORKING AT ASOS MUST BE REALLY EXCITING — IS IT AS YOU EXPECTED? Working at ASOS isn't how I ever imagined my first job would be. It's very exciting and a genuinely fun place to work. I think that we all find it exciting to work for a company that is not like any other out there at the moment. At first it did take me a while to adjust to the concept that we have no physical shop or store, as it is an unusual set-up in the fashion industry. I think that I'm really lucky to have joined the company at the time I did, as this year is our 10th birthday. As someone new to the business it's great to be looking back at where ASOS has come over the last 10 years and the plans for what happens next.

WHICH PRODUCT CATEGORIES DO YOU WORK ON?

My department is Womenswear Branded and Premium Accessories so I work on all women's accessories on the website which do not have the ASOS label. This covers all accessories categories with the exception of footwear and jewellery, so I work on handbags, purses, sunglasses, scarves, hats, hosiery, and many more.

WHAT DOES YOUR ROLE INVOLVE ON A DAILY BASIS?

My job changes on a daily basis but, in basic terms, I provide the administrative support for my Buyer and Assistant Buyer. On our team there are just the three of us and my role very much revolves around our samples. As I work on the branded side of the business I don't get involved in product development; instead, our buyer picks exactly the styles she wants from our designers or brands. Once she has placed the order it is my job to confirm this with the supplier and then raise it on our system. Once the official order is on the system, I have to chase a sample of each style in each colour on our order because we need to photo-shoot every product.

Unlike another business where there is a physical shop, we are only able to present our product on the internet so the samples are required for a model photo-shoot, a still photo-shoot, a catwalk video (clothing only) and a 360 degree shot (accessories only).

It's also part of my job to work closely with the production team to organise the photo-shoot process so that when product is delivered to our warehouse we have all the necessary imagery for the product to go live on the website and be sold. I then also use the samples to give to our press office and our magazine and newsletter teams for them to help publicise our product.

My day does also involve a lot of problem solving and troubleshooting with our brands to make sure all our processes are running as smoothly as possible.

HOW DO YOU ACTUALLY DECIDE ON WHICH STYLES TO CHOOSE – WHAT IS THE PROCESS?

This part of the job is not something I get very involved with at my level. This is left more to my Buyer and Assistant Buyer, although I have been given the opportunity to attend buying appointments and give my opinion.

WHO DO YOU REPORT TO, AND WHO ELSE DO YOU LIAISE WITH?

My team is quite small, including my Buyer and Assistant Buyer who I report to. I also work with our Merchandising team and Production team, and speak with many of our suppliers on a daily basis as I'm one of their main points of contact.

Faye looking foxy!

Here to answer your questions about getting into buying are Faye Bamber from ASOS (read our interview with her on the previous page) and Emma Clark from 24 Seven, London.

Emma Clark: London-based Emma is a Recruitment Consultant for the buying and merchandising division with leading fashion recruitment agency 24 Seven, where she finds top talent for clients such as Topshop, All Saints, Ted Baker and The Body Shop. She is a real buying expert, having spent eight years as a buyer with companies such as Dorothy Perkins, MKOne and Bay Trading.

WHAT DOES A BUYER DO IN AN AVERAGE DAY?

That is the great thing about fashion buying, no two days are the same. Generally speaking though, your week will start off with the analysis of the previous week's sales. If you have had a great week, then your focus will be building on this and chasing in more stock to keep the good sales going. However, if you have had a poor week's sales, then your focus should be on how to overcome and improve on this.

The rest of the week will be full of supplier appointments, competitive shopping (where you go to your competitors' shops to see what they are up to), internal meetings and sourcing new and exciting product for your range.
EMMA CLARK

HOW DO BUYERS PREDICT WHAT CONSUMERS WANT?

This involves a lot of analysis. Buyers will analyse past years' product ranges and look at best and worst sellers to determine the possible outcome of new ranges. This will involve analysing selling price, colour, shape, fabric, etc. Buyers will also look at future trends coming through on the catwalks to determine consumers' future needs and wants.
EMMA CLARK

WOULD YOU SAY THAT MOST PEOPLE WHO WORK IN BUYING HAVE A DEGREE?

Most of the people I know in buying at ASOS and other similar companies do have a degree, but these are all in different areas of fashion and sometimes people have degrees in other subjects apart from fashion too.
FAYE BAMBER

An industry-related/specialist degree will definitely help get your foot in the door, e.g. Fashion & Textiles, Fashion Buying & Merchandising etc. However, this is not essential. I got my foot in the door of Arcadia with a Spanish & Business degree — I just happened

to be so OBSESSED with fashion and determined to make it my career that they gave me the job!
EMMA CLARK

HOW DO BUYERS DECIDE ON WHAT PRODUCT TO BUY? DO THEY VISIT TRADE SHOWS TO FIND NEW PRODUCT?

Buyers have to look at a lot of different factors to help them decide what product to buy. These include past product performance and current and future trends. They then have to consider what colour, print, fabric, trims, etc will be involved in the product and at what price to retail the product at, all the while relating this back to the customers' needs and wants. Buyers also visit trade shows and fairs and try to attend inspiration shopping trips, as well as sourcing trips, to determine the best product to develop and select for the range.
EMMA CLARK

WHAT DOES IT FEEL LIKE, KNOWING THAT YOU CAN DETERMINE WHAT PEOPLE WILL BE WEARING?

I find it really exciting once the appointments and orders for our next season begin to come in and, especially with our designer product, seeing the styles that have been on the catwalks coming into stock, or even seeing the product of new designers. In my role it's great once all the new product arrives so I can suggest it to our newsletter, press or magazine to use in editorials and style advice.
FAYE BAMBER

HOW MANY TIMES A YEAR DOES A BUYER SELECT NEW PRODUCT — IS IT SIMPLY SPRING/SUMMER AND AUTUMN/WINTER?

Budgets are broken down into the two seasons, spring/summer and autumn/winter, and then further broken down into months. Generally speaking a buyer will be buying new product throughout the year, as they normally buy the ranges one month at a time.
EMMA CLARK

Image: Sally McEntyre c/o Bestseller

WHAT HAPPENS ON A BUYING TRIP?

This entirely depends on whether it is a sourcing trip or an inspirational trip. On an inspirational buying trip, buyers will visit fashion hotspots of the world and go shopping to find inspiration for the hottest new trends (basically you are shopping and getting paid to do it). However, it's not all glamour. Often you're very limited in time and you have to spend all day, every day on your feet, traipsing around shops. Once you're back on home soil, you then need to put together a report on what you saw, in conjunction with the garments that you bought and present this to your buying manager and the rest of your team.

On a sourcing trip, your focus is completely different. Along with your designer, you will visit suppliers and their factories and develop product for sampling. This is fun but also extremely tiring, as the work normally starts the second you step off the plane.
EMMA CLARK

WHAT ADVICE WOULD YOU GIVE TO STUDENTS WHO ARE LOOKING TO GET INTO BUYING?

I don't think that it is necessarily important that you have studied buying, as the fact I had studied design didn't cause me any problems.

I think that the most important thing is that you have done work experience in a buying role so that you know what the environment is and that it is right for you. But I do also think it's important to get as much experience in all areas of the industry as possible because not only does it aid your choice when choosing your career path, it also makes you better informed about the industry as a whole.
FAYE BAMBER

You will definitely need a lot of determination to succeed in this industry – if at first you don't succeed, try, try (you know how it goes). Above all, you have to be extremely passionate and

enthusiastic about making fashion buying your life. It is not an easy road to begin with, and none too glamorous either, so you really need that hunger and drive to see you through.
EMMA CLARK

WHAT ARE THE PERKS OF BEING A BUYER?

If you work for a large high-street retailer you tend to get a discount in store — yay! You also meet lots of interesting people and travel to exciting places. Another perk is getting invited to sample sales, where clothes are either free or very cheap. I used to come home with bin bags full of stuff at the beginning of my career — something that my other half did not appreciate.
EMMA CLARK

HOW DOES THE BUYING DEPARTMENT KNOW WHAT WILL SELL AND WHAT WON'T? ARE THERE PROCESSES YOU GO THROUGH TO DETERMINE THIS?

We review our sales every week in our 'best and worst' reports and presentations on a Monday morning, so this gives us a regular update on what is selling and what is not. The strategy of what we buy for the next season is usually determined by my Buyer and Merchandiser, along with the heads of department.
FAYE BAMBER

DO YOU HAVE TO BE GOOD AT MATHS TO BE A BUYER?

You don't have to be a whizz, but being proficient at maths definitely helps, as there is a fair amount of analysis and calculating that goes on in buying.
EMMA CLARK

DO MOST BUYERS WORK ON ONE PARTICULAR PRODUCT AREA, OR ACROSS MANY DIFFERENT PRODUCTS?

This entirely depends on the type and size of company that you work for. Generally speaking, the larger the company you work for, the more likely you are to look after just one product area, e.g. denim. The smaller the company, the more likely you are to look after multiple areas, e.g. casual, which can consist of denim, casual bottoms, casual tops, etc.
EMMA CLARK

WHAT WOULD WORK EXPERIENCE IN A BUYING OFFICE INVOLVE — WHAT SORT OF TASKS WOULD STUDENTS BE ALLOCATED?

The tasks that would be allocated to students on work experience are normally fairly administrative in nature. So you may be asked to help with the filing of orders or fabric swatches for example, or you could be asked to help organise the sample cupboard. Any experience that you can get is invaluable as, regardless of what you are asked to do, you will be able to soak up the atmosphere of a buying office and gain an insight into how it all works.
EMMA CLARK

HOW CAN STUDENTS WHO ARE STILL AT SCHOOL OR COLLEGE BEGIN TO PREPARE FOR A CAREER IN BUYING — IS THERE ANYTHING THEY CAN BE DOING NOW?

They can apply for short internships or work experience. If you are not studying on a buying- or fashion-related degree or course, then try and learn as much about the industry as possible in your spare time. Know your onions! If you want to succeed in fashion, you need to live, breathe and sleep it. Know the current and future trends inside out. Keep an eye out for what is happening on the high street and know your designers. The more fashion mags you read the better, and *Drapers* is a good trade magazine to subscribe to for the inside track.
EMMA CLARK

Image: Sally McEntyre c/o Bestseller

To Do List

▶ **GO SHOPPING** without spending. Visit different shops in your area to compare and contrast each one and establish what's good about their product range and what could be improved. Find out their pricing structure (does the store offer value for money or is it over-priced?). This is called doing a shop report, and you should keep notes of your findings for future reference, and also do a new one each season. Choose three or four stores to report on each time, which are all quite similar. So, you could select trend-led retailers Topshop, River Island, Miss Selfridge and H&M for one report. Or you might compare and contrast department stores, such as John Lewis, Debenhams and House of Fraser. Visiting department stores will also give you the opportunity to discover lots of different products, as they stock so many collections from lots of different brands. Collect any brochures, leaflets and in-store magazines from shops you visit, to help you understand more about each brand.

Over time, you will be able to give an opinion on which stores have the best/ most interesting product mix and why, and which ones aren't so successful. This information will really help once you begin being interviewed for buying courses at college or uni, or go for work experience interviews. You will be expected to relay this information and have an idea of who is doing well on the high street, and be able to explain who your favourite designers and brands are (and why).

▶ **RESEARCH** online – you don't even have to leave the house to find out about exciting brands and designers. There are so many really good online stores, which often give profiles on the designers they stock so you can learn as you view the products. Good ones to look at are:
www.netaporter.com
www.matchesfashion.com
www.my-wardrobe.com
www.asos.com

VERO MODA

IN THIS CHAPTER:

"The creative aspect of the job can be very subjective – there's no right or wrong way of doing things, so you have to trust your own creative judgment when working on a project."

Elpida Magkoura, Freelance Visual Merchandiser

Top to bottom) VM: Elpida Magkoura, c/o John Smedley, VM: Sally McEntyre, c/o Bestseller

WHAT DOES A VISUAL MERCHANDISER DO?

A visual merchandiser's (VM) job is to arrange the product sold in a shop, make it look more desirable to buy and create a distinctive identity for the brand they work with. The aim is to attract people into a store with exciting displays and to make their shopping experience as interesting as possible, ultimately resulting in more sales.

Most people think that a VM just focuses on window dressing, but this is only a small part of the job. VMs are responsible for the overall look of the whole store, from organising graphics and signage, to creating promotional material for in-store events, and coming up with concepts to make the store stand out from its competitors at busy periods such as at sale time and Christmas.

Their role can be hugely varied and involve working on lots of different brands and products, including womenswear, menswear, kidswear, accessories and homeware (experienced VMs might specialise in one or two product areas later in their career).

Responsibilities vary depending on experience level. A junior VM will be very hands-on, dressing mannequins, arranging product on the shop floor, and assisting in sourcing and making props, while a more senior VM or head of display is more office-based, designing the displays, managing the organisation of the department and staff training. VM directors for large brands may also oversee operations on a global or national level.

WHO EMPLOYS VISUAL MERCHANDISERS?

Most retailers have at least one specialist visual merchandiser, while the majority of medium to large stores have a team of VMs (some companies employ up to 50 people in this sector). Employers include department stores such as Selfridges, retail chains like Topshop, and high-end luxury boutiques like Louis Vuitton. Smaller stores might rely on sales assistants to work on VM instead of hiring specialists, if their budget is small. A few VMs also work for e-tailers (online retailers). While most people work full-time in this sector, there are also freelance opportunities for senior VMs, where they work with a couple of different clients.

KEY WORKING RELATIONSHIPS

A typical VM team is managed by a head of department, who in turn reports to the creative director, the marketing director or the CEO. A larger team will have head office-based VMs and also store-based VMs.

The visual merchandisers work closely with all other departments — they need to interact with the buyers and merchandisers, the marketing and PR team and the retail operation team, as well as with store managers and sales staff from each store they're responsible for.

RELATED ROLES

Most VMs stay within this sector as a long-term career. The skills acquired could also transfer to set/exhibition design, interior design or styling, while some people may progress from a senior VM position to the role of a creative director (usually if they have worked within the same brand for a long time).

WORKING HOURS

Most full-time VMs work 9–5, Monday to Friday, but many stores require their teams to work outside shop-opening hours, especially if working on window displays. VMs will also be expected to work longer hours at key times such as before the first day of a sale and at Christmas.

SALARY

For a London-based VM the entry-level salary is approximately £16k–£20k. A head of VM can earn more than £50k, while a lucky few can reach the £100k mark.

EDUCATION:

Useful school/sixth form subjects: Art, Media Studies, Textiles, Graphics, IT, Fashion

It's not essential to have specialist qualifications to work in visual merchandising, as many people work their way up within a company from sales or other store-based roles or come from general fashion courses. However, this is a competitive area, so you may want to consider a specialist course to boost your CV.

- London College of Communication: Introduction to Display & Visual Merchandising (one-day course)
- Berkshire College: Various short courses by the British Display Society (www.britishdisplaysociety.co.uk)
- London College of Fashion: Foundation Degree Fashion Retail Branding & Visual Merchandising

BEST THINGS ABOUT THE JOB

- The role can be very creative (once you become more senior) and loads of fun
- You are helping a brand to become more profitable through producing effective visuals and a strong brand identity
- It can be great to work with a strong team of like-minded people and see a concept grow from initial idea to installation
- There is a huge variety of responsibilities, so the job isn't repetitive

WORST THINGS ABOUT THE JOB

- The pay can be low until you get to a senior level
- The hours are long and you need to work overnight when there are big installations to finish
- Trends in visuals change very quickly, so you have to constantly keep ahead of everyone else
- You're only as good as the last project you worked on, so there's a lot of pressure to get it right on every job you do

WHAT SKILLS ARE NEEDED TO BE A VISUAL MERCHANDISER?

- Creative flair
- Some DIY skills — knowing how to paint or use a drill will come in very handy
- Knowledge of graphics and strong computer skills can be an advantage
- Good eye for detail
- Good presentation skills — both verbal, written and visual
- Confidence and self-motivation
- Excellent knowledge of fashion brands and trends, and strong commercial awareness

Image: VM: Sally McEntyre, c/o Bestseller

Elpida is a freelance VM specialising in the luxury fashion sector. She's based in London and works with British and international brands, covering all aspects of visual merchandising for in-store displays, windows and events. Elpida has been in the business for more than 10 years and has held full-time VM roles with Selfridges, Giorgio Armani, Jaeger and Net-A-Porter. You can see her work at www.visualmerchandising.co.uk

EDUCATION
School: Elpida finished school in Athens, Greece, having completed the equivalent of A-levels
College: Two-year diploma in Fashion Design in Athens
University: BA in Fashion Design at University of Westminster

Industry Insider!

WHAT MADE YOU DECIDE TO GET INTO VISUAL MERCHANDISING?
After I graduated I needed a job to pay the rent and I was working as a department manager in Selfridges, London. I was dying to do something more creative and when I saw a vacancy within the VM department in Selfridges I applied for the role. I got the job and loved it.

WHAT DO YOU GET UP TO IN AN AVERAGE DAY?
In my role as a freelance VM I get to do a bit of everything, which is great. Each day is different, but generally my work entails designing concepts, project managing their implementation and delivering the installation. I can be doing anything from finding props, dressing mannequins, sketching ideas, to having meetings with the client.

DO YOU SKETCH OUT YOUR IDEAS BEFORE YOU PUT THEM INTO PRACTICE – DO YOU HAVE TO CREATE A PROPER ILLUSTRATION?
Yes, when it comes to designing a concept (i.e. a window display) VMs will always have to present the idea to the head of the department or the client to get the go-ahead for the project. They need to provide detailed illustrations of the concept to show how they envisage the end result. Most VMs use CAD programs to help them illustrate their ideas, which takes less time than hand sketching and provides a clearer and more realistic result.

YOU'VE ALSO DONE ONLINE VM – HOW DOES THAT WORK, AND HOW DIFFERENT IS IT TO DOING TRADITIONAL VM?
Online VM is very different to store-based VM. I would say that an online VM is a stylist who also needs to have the commercial thinking of a visual merchandiser. Online shopping is still a relatively new way of shopping and in my opinion it is underdeveloped in terms of product presentation. I think this will change with the advances of technology, which will create opportunities to become more creative in this area.

WHAT DOES NO ONE TELL YOU BEFORE YOU START OUT IN THIS BUSINESS?
When you work for a company, everyone within that company will have an opinion on VM! Be prepared to receive criticism from all departments within a business. The creative aspect of the job can be very subjective – there's no right or wrong way of doing things, so you have to trust your own creative judgment when working on a project.

Elpida

Image: VM: Elpida Magkoura, c/o John Smedley

Images: VM: Elpida Magkoura, c/o Yellow Door

Sally McEntyre is UK Country Manager for Visual Merchandising & Marketing with leading Danish fashion group Bestseller, where she's responsible for five brands — Jack & Jones, Vero Moda, ONLY, Pieces and Name It. She has more than 12 years of experience in creative display, and her CV boasts some of the most well-known fashion retailers, including River Island, Kookai, M&S and Morgan.

EDUCATION
A-levels: Art, English Literature, History of Art
College: National Diploma in Art & Design at West Cheshire College, Chester
University: BA degree in Textile Design at University of Leeds

Industry Insider!

WHAT MADE YOU DECIDE TO GET INTO VISUAL MERCHANDISING? Well, I sort of fell into it really. After uni I had no idea what I wanted to do as a career, so went off travelling to India for a year. Unfortunately I had an accident, ended up coming home early and moved back in with my parents. After a while they were keen for me to begin looking for work, so I went to the job centre to see what was on offer. The first thing they told me about was a visual merchandising job at Marks & Spencer, where I was interviewed, got the role, and stayed there for two years.

THAT'S GREAT THAT IT HAPPENED SO QUICKLY...
I know, I was kind of lucky. I didn't have a portfolio of work demonstrating any visual merchandising work, although I did have my work from uni, so I had to rely on being able to show them my understanding of fashion verbally when I went for the interview and I think they liked my personality. At that time, visual merchandising was nowhere near as competitive as it is now — these days it's much tougher at interview stage.

WHAT'S IT REALLY LIKE WORKING IN VISUAL MERCHANDISING? It's not as creative as you might expect in the beginning — the brand you work for will dictate exactly how they want the displays to be, and you will be expected to follow strict guidelines to adhere to the corporate identity. This is done by following rules in what are called style guides: each brand or retailer will have a book outlining how signage should be positioned, how mannequins are to be displayed and so on, so that all of the stores look cohesive and have an easily recognisable identity. As you become more senior in your career you will have the opportunity to become more creative, but you have to have a natural talent and flair to be given the opportunity to push the boundaries.

WHAT'S BEEN THE MOST EXCITING POINT IN YOUR CAREER? It was when I worked for River Island and was promoted from Senior Visual Merchandiser to the role of Visual Display Manager, where I was responsible for giving direction and overseeing the windows and in-store display for all 250 stores. I was working directly with the MD to brainstorm new ideas and concepts, and had lots more responsibility and freedom to develop my own ideas than I'd ever had before.

Smiley Sal

All images: VM: Sally McEntyre, c/o Bestseller

Elpida Magkoura and Sally McEntyre from the previous pages answer your questions on getting into visual merchandising.

IS VISUAL MERCHANDISING A DIFFICULT CAREER TO GET INTO?

I don't think so, but you have to really want it and you should be prepared to start with a very low salary.
ELPIDA MAGKOURA

It's much harder than it used to be – there's more competition, so you have to really stand out from the crowd.
SALLY McENTYRE

HOW CREATIVE IS THIS TYPE OF ROLE? DO YOU GET A LOT OF FREEDOM TO DO WHAT YOU WANT?

How creative the job is depends on the company you work for and of course your role within the department. Every company has its own brand guidelines which all the creative departments have to follow. Most companies also have specific visual merchandising guidelines. If we look at the role of a VM responsible for dressing windows, some companies will encourage creativity from the individual within the given guidelines and others will want you to just strictly follow those guidelines (dressing and positioning props and mannequins in the window exactly as per the photograph provided). The larger the company is, the stricter the guidelines usually are.
ELPIDA MAGKOURA

WHERE ARE THE BEST PLACES TO FIND INSPIRATION?

The best places to get inspired are in little independent boutiques and smaller brands, where they really push the boundaries and have a lot of scope to be creative. At the other end of the scale, major department stores such as Harvey Nichols, Liberty and Selfridges in London always have interesting displays.
SALLY McENTYRE

HOW DO VMs FIND JOBS? IS IT VIA HEADHUNTERS OR IS IT MORE WORD-OF-MOUTH?

Most companies will advertise their VM positions via their websites and also on retail job opportunities websites. A lot of companies will brief a recruitment agency to find the right person for the position.
ELPIDA MAGKOURA

People also network a lot – this is a very close-knit sector of the industry, where everyone knows each other, and you're constantly making new contacts.
SALLY McENTYRE

IS BEING A WINDOW DRESSER THE SAME AS BEING A VM?

Window dressing is only part of the duties of a VM. A lot of people are not familiar with the term visual merchandiser and would refer to a visual merchandiser as a window dresser.
ELPIDA MAGKOURA

WHAT SHOULD A PROSPECTIVE VM HAVE IN THEIR PORTFOLIO?

Once you start working it is important to document your work (take photographs) and present those in a portfolio. This will help you get your next job. Remember that how you dress yourself will say a lot about your work too (if you can't style yourself I wouldn't feel confident in your ability to be able to style mannequins).
ELPIDA MAGKOURA

WHAT ARE YOUR TOP TIPS FOR SOMEONE WHO WANTS TO GET INTO VISUAL MERCHANDISING?

When going for work experience, try to focus on the stores you can really relate to, as you must be able to show an interest, knowledge and excitement for the brand you interview with. Also, begin to style your friends so you get the hang of putting outfits and looks together and you will feel more confident when you do your work experience. Think of your friends as walking mannequins!
SALLY McENTYRE

HOW CAN YOUNG PEOPLE PREPARE FOR A CAREER IN VM – WHAT PRACTICAL THINGS COULD THEY BE DOING NOW IN PREPARATION FOR WORK EXPERIENCE OR TO ENTER FASHION EDUCATION?

Start to keep a photographic diary of all the things that inspire you when you're out and about. These can be as diverse as stores you see on holiday, people at festivals, window displays you like. Begin to practise doing comparative shop reports of the stores in your area. These should note what the store does well in terms of display, what it doesn't do well,

what you like and don't like about how it presents its displays and visuals, plus type of graphics and signage it uses. Your reports should be mainly visual (photos and sketches) with text alongside. Choose stores that are similar to each other so you can compare and contrast them – e.g. Topshop, River Island and Hennes or Marks & Spencer, BHS and Next.
SALLY McENTYRE

You should learn about fashion designers, brands and retailers – become as informed as possible on all these things. Also, visit shops (designer and high-street) and study the in-store displays and windows.
ELPIDA MAGKOURA

BASED ON THE PEOPLE YOU KNOW WHO WORK IN VM, WOULD YOU SAY IT'S ESSENTIAL TO HAVE A FORMAL QUALIFICATION OR DEGREE TO WORK IN VM, OR CAN SOMEONE WORK THEIR WAY UP FROM THE SHOPFLOOR?
Yes, it's definitely possible to work your way up if you've already worked on the retail sales side of the business. Although some people train on specialist courses, I believe that having a flair for VM comes from natural talent and it can't always be taught. You either have it or you don't. Regardless of what

qualifications someone has, what I'm looking for when I interview is a great personality, good attitude and some previous work experience. All these things are more important than a qualification.
SALLY McENTYRE

Most people I know that work in VM have worked their way up. It's not essential to have formal qualifications. However, higher education is not something that you do just to get a job – it develops you personally and it's an experience I wouldn't want to have missed.
ELPIDA MAGKOURA

IF SOMEONE STARTS THEIR CAREER WORKING FOR A HIGH-STREET RETAILER, IS IT THEN DIFFICULT TO TRANSFER TO WORKING IN THE LUXURY SECTOR?
It isn't easy to transfer from high street to luxury. Most luxury brands will require you to have experience in the luxury sector to consider you for a position. If you would like to specialise in the luxury sector make sure your first job is in the luxury sector, so you're starting as you mean to go on.
ELPIDA MAGKOURA

Image: VM: Elpida Magkoura, c/o Yellow Door

Image: VM: Sally McEntyre, c/o Bestseller

To Do List

▶ **START** an ideas or reference scrap book of things you find inspirational — whenever you're out and about take your camera and notebook so you can document exciting window displays, mannequins or people who have an unusual style. This reference book will come in useful for ideas once you begin university, work experience or a proper role.

▶ **GET** some work experience. Send your CV to as many different stores in your area as possible, and try a mixture of shops to gain experience working in different environments. Working for a large corporate retailer will differ quite a lot from working for a small boutique. Also offer your services to charity shops for free — you might gain some great hands-on experience working for them, as the majority will be hugely appreciative of someone offering to do this role. If you already have a job working as a sales assistant within a fashion store, you have the ideal opportunity to ask your employers if you can also help out occasionally doing VM.

▶ **RESEARCH** as many websites as possible to gain inspiration and learn more about the industry. Elpida Magkoura recommends the following sites:
www.vmsd.com
www.rvmww.com
www.anothernormal.com

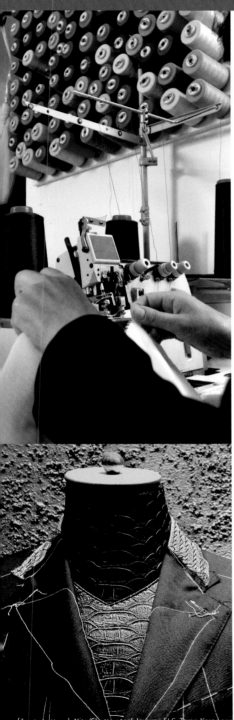

IN THIS CHAPTER:

"It's so rewarding when your ideas become best-sellers and you've been able to follow the design from concept to final product."

Paul Corben, Senior Product Developer

[Top to bottom]: Nito/Shutterstock Images LLC, Zoran Karapancev/Shutterstock Images LLC

WHAT DO THESE ROLES INVOLVE?

The production and technical side of the industry is huge and very diverse, offering opportunities for people who want to work in the fashion industry but who don't necessarily want to go down a more mainstream route such as design or styling. This sector is much more practical and hands-on – the design side provides the ideas, while production and technical staff ensure that those ideas are actually feasible and get them from paper to real products. Without production and technical staff, products would never see the light of day – they ensure that patterns are correct, develop and test fabrics and trims, make sure that the fit of garments/accessories is accurate, sew and embellish the product, work in and liaise with factories, and oversee product and fabric innovations. There so many different roles that we haven't been able to cover all of them, so in the interview section we have focused on three key areas – product development, garment technology and pattern cutting.

WHO EMPLOYS PRODUCTION STAFF?

Opportunities exist for production and technical staff in all market levels and sectors of the fashion industry. They could be working in house for a brand, couture company or high-street retailer, where the majority work in a studio, or they could be working for a factory, supplier or manufacturer. Most work full-time, but there are lots of freelance roles for pattern cutters and machinists in particular.

KEY WORKING RELATIONSHIPS

Production/technical staff generally report to a department manager, such as head of production, pattern room manager, or product development manager. In addition to their direct colleagues, they will spend most of their time liaising with factories, suppliers and fabric mills. They will provide invaluable support to the design team, advising them of any parts of the design that might be problematic and helping work out how to make improvements.

RELATED ROLES

Production and technical staff often begin their careers in another sector of the industry, including design, sales, buying or merchandising, and some transfer back to these roles after a career in technical/production roles. However, it's important that they keep their skills up to date. For instance, to go back into a design role, they would have to provide an updated portfolio demonstrating an understanding of up-coming trends and showing that they are still able to sketch and present ideas well.

WORKING HOURS

Standard hours are approximately 40 hours per week, but this can vary if employees are either spending time overseas on factory visits or working late to meet deadlines. For example, it is very common for pattern cutters, seamstresses and machinists who are employed by couture or luxury labels to work through the night to finish collections in the run-up to the catwalk shows each season.

SALARY

While salaries generally start off quite low – approximately £14k–18k depending on location (with the figure being considerably higher if based in London or another major fashion capital) – employees can expect to earn much more as they become more senior, especially if they are trained in a specialist sector such as Gerber pattern cutting. Don't assume that the high salaries are only paid in the design or buying sector – production and technical staff can command up to £80k at a senior level.

Image: Paul Corben

EDUCATION:

Useful school/college subjects: Art, Design & Technology, Product Design, Textiles, Fashion

In the past, lots of production staff have worked their way up within companies without having specialist qualifications, and some have come from other sectors of the industry. However, as competition for positions increases, it will look good on your CV if you have studied a specialist course at college or university – these will often give you the opportunity to make important contacts via course-related work experience. Here are a few courses to consider (bear in mind that you don't always need to have done a fashion course – some people come from backgrounds in product design too):

- Northumbria University (London campus): BA (Hons) Fashion Product Management
- De Montfort University (Leicester): BSc (Hons) Fashion Technology
- Cardonald College (Glasgow): HND Fashion Technology
- Manchester Metropolitan University: BA (Hons) Fashion Design & Technology

BEST THINGS ABOUT THE JOB

- The buzz of seeing a product in store and selling well
- Travel overseas and seeing new cultures
- Meeting new people
- Being challenged and also constantly giving and receiving knowledge and information, ensuring you're always learning something new

WORST THINGS ABOUT THE JOB

- Finding a factory you would like to work with to develop your product, but then realising they are too expensive to use
- Bad deliveries – when product arrives back from the factories and isn't as expected
- Working with designers who have little commercial knowledge and trying to interpret their requirements

WHAT SKILLS ARE NEEDED TO WORK IN PRODUCTION/TECHNICAL?

- A creative and commercial eye
- Ability to meet deadlines
- Pattern cutting and garment construction knowledge
- Good sewing skills
- Knowledge of fabric characteristics
- Good maths skills – an advantage when it comes to calculating complex measurements

Image: Nito/Shutterstock Images LLC

Paul Corben is a Senior Product Developer with more than 25 years of industry experience. Based in the UK, Paul has worked across many sectors within fashion, specialising in accessories, including footwear, bags, belts, small leather goods, jewellery, hosiery and luggage. He began his career in footwear retail, going on to work in senior positions in sales and buying with major brands and suppliers and also in various consultancy roles.

Industry Insider

WHAT MADE YOU DECIDE TO GET INTO THE TECHNICAL SIDE OF FASHION?
My first job in fashion was with a French footwear retailer. While working on the shop-floor in front of the final customer, I was always interested in knowing more about how the shoes were developed and constructed in order to be able to respond directly to any queries they had about the product. That led to an interest in the product development side of the industry.

DID YOU DO WORK EXPERIENCE IN THIS SECTOR WHEN YOU WERE STILL AT COLLEGE. IF SO, WHERE, AND WHAT DID IT INVOLVE?
I grew up with a father who was involved in men's shoe manufacture, so I visited factories and trade exhibitions from an early age, and caught the bug. I suppose that was my work experience – learning and questioning things as I went along.

WHAT DOES AN AVERAGE DAY INVOLVE?
No two days are the same, but a day might involve liaising with all number of departments in house from design, to buying, marketing and accounts. The majority of time is spent liaising with factories overseas and making sure the critical path is on course and everything is running smoothly.

WHAT'S THE MOST CHALLENGING ASPECT OF WORKING IN PRODUCT DEVELOPMENT?
Getting the right product at the right quality and price is always a challenge but that's par for the course for the role of a product developer. And, of course, it can be challenging making sure the product is completed and delivered on time.

IS THIS AN EXCITING CAREER CHOICE?
Yes, I would say so. If you're looking for a job that offers constant activity, challenges and stimulation, then it's a good option. Depending on the company you work for, there's the opportunity for lots of overseas travel (to trade fairs, and to visit factories and suppliers). You will also get to meet lots of new and creative people, as the role involves liaison with many skilled crafts people, designers and product makers. This role is also very rewarding when your ideas become bestsellers, and you've been able to follow the design from concept through to final product – seeing your product in store is exciting.

IS PRODUCT DEVELOPMENT CREATIVE OR NOT?
It depends on the company you work for – it can be. I know of some who just take someone else's idea and give it mechanically to a factory to produce. Personally I get very involved with the creative side and enjoy the buzz of being involved from concept to consumer.

Paul looking cheery!

Images: Paul Corben

London-based June Lawrence is a Garment Technologist for the SC51 menswear brand (part of World Design & Trade Ltd). She's been in the industry for 10 years, and has also worked for John Lewis, French Connection and Ted Baker, specialising in menswear.

EDUCATION:
College: June attended Bilston College and studied A-level Fashion, Dressmaking and Art
University: BA (Hons) Fashion at University of Central Lancashire

Industry Insider!

HOW DID YOU WORK YOUR WAY UP TO THE ROLE YOU HAVE NOW? WHAT OTHER ROLES HAVE YOU WORKED IN?

I was firstly a Junior Designer, straight out of university, which I enjoyed greatly. Then I did both design and pattern cutting and moved into managing a number of design rooms in the West End of London. After being made redundant from one of these particular roles, which I had been in for five years, I noticed a garment tech role in the *Evening Standard*. The skills that I had picked up along the way all came to the fore and fortunately the company offered me training on the fabric it specialised in, which was leather.

WHAT MADE YOU DECIDE TO GET INTO GARMENT TECHNOLOGY SPECIFICALLY?

As I'd worked in designing and pattern cutting in the past, I wanted to combine both areas with a more technical bias, while still being in the fashion industry. The role mentioned above combined all the skills I had already acquired and seemed ideal – I was lucky enough to be offered the job within a week of applying.

WHAT DOES AN AVERAGE DAY INVOLVE?

As with most people, e-mails are the first thing to deal with, as the time difference between here and the factories overseas (often in the Far East) can cause delays unless all e-mails get a quick response. Then, depending on the design cycle we happen to be in, I could either be working on protos (initial samples to check fits) or salesman samples (samples the sales agents use to sell our range, which are developed in the proper fabrics) and production samples (what should be the last sample to confirm fit, fabric and all accessories).

Within any of these phases, I could either be creating specification sheets (which tell the factory exactly what the crucial measurements should be), or attending a fit meeting. The latter involves organising a fit model, for a session where all the clothes that need fitting are shown to all parties concerned to assess the garments one by one, and make amendments where necessary). If I'm attending fit meetings, I am responsible for improving fits and making suggestions where needed. And, if I'm involved in production issues and returns, I resolve them straight away to prevent any loss of sales.

WHAT'S THE MOST CHALLENGING ASPECT OF YOUR ROLE?

The most challenging aspect of my job is trying to satisfy everyone with regards to fit and silhouettes. Sometimes the designer wants something that may not be that practical or affordable and it is my responsibility to consider a suitable compromise that gives the desired effect, but is also both achievable and practical.

IF YOU START OUT IN GARMENT TECH, IS IT EASY TO TRANSFER INTO ACCESSORIES TECH?

All the skills you develop and learn can definitely be transferred over to other specialist areas, including accessories.

HOW MUCH TRAVEL IS INVOLVED IN THIS TYPE OF ROLE, AND WHAT'S INVOLVED IN A TRIP? Generally I would get to travel to different factories to examine their production facilities and processes and ensure they follow our health and safety requirements and labour laws. It's our job to make sure no child or adult is exploited in the making of our clothes, for instance. However, the set-up at the company I work for at the moment, SC51, provides agents who cover that aspect of the job, which means I am not taken out of the studio for lengthy periods – a more cost-effective approach.

Images: June Lawrence, c/o WDT

HOW MANY PEOPLE WORK WITHIN A GARMENT TECH TEAM? HOW IS THE TEAM STRUCTURED? There's usually a team of garment technologists, headed by a senior manager who oversees the department. The workload is generally divided up in two ways: by product area – knitted or woven – or by gender and ages, e.g. ladies-, mens- or childrenswear. In my particular situation, as it is a single-gender brand, I work alone and cover all the product areas.

Based in London, Ann Watson is a Senior Pattern Cutter for AllSaints. She began her career as a designer with Zandra Rhodes, going on to work with high-street retailers such as Monsoon as well as high-end, luxury brands. Ann also had her own womenswear label for 15 years.

EDUCATION:
BA Fashion Design & Technology at Newcastle Polytechnic (now Northumbria University)

WHAT MADE YOU DECIDE TO GET INTO PATTERN CUTTING?

Although I trained in design and went on to work as a designer for many years, I had always enjoyed the pattern-cutting and -making side of the job. Following a career in womenswear, I stopped full-time work for five years when my son was little, and when the time came to go back into the industry I decided to focus on the pattern-cutting side, which to me seemed slightly less stressful than working on design. That's not to say that pattern cutting isn't stressful. It's just that design comes with a different type of stress, and there are so many other people vying for the same roles, that it's much more competitive. Pattern cutting seemed a good outlet for my skills, and I've never looked back.

WHAT PRODUCT AREA DO YOU SPECIALISE IN?

I've always specialised in womenswear. At the moment I work solely on premium product – the 'red carpet' type of dress, which includes eveningwear and long gowns, with lots of attention to detail. Because it's a special product with intricate patterns, these pieces take quite a long time to create – I could be working on one pattern for three or four days in a row, uninterrupted. The workmanship and special fabrics are reflected in the price, with dresses retailing at £100–£450. I used to work on couture/designer-level product at high-end label Amanda Wakeley, which is where I learned to work on these types of complicated and detailed garments.

WHAT DOES AN AVERAGE DAY INVOLVE?

At the beginning of each day, the pattern-cutting team is assigned work by the Design Director, the Pattern Room Manager or their assistant. Each pattern cutter will be given a work sheet with a brief of what is involved in and expected for each garment. I'm a manual pattern cutter, which means I do everything by hand rather than on the computer and I do all of my work on the stand. This involves a mannequin, so I'm constantly working in 3D and creating the pattern pieces on a body shape, rather than in flat format. Once a mock-up of the garment has been created in calico (called a toile), we will do fit sessions with a model to see if the piece looks good on a real body, and make amendments so it looks as good as possible.

Other people in the team then put any amendments into the computer system and digitise the piece using computer-aided design and manufacture systems (CAD/CAM) such as Gerber or Lectra. This means that the pattern pieces are input into the computer so changes and measurements can be made quickly and easily and the pattern can be sent electronically to our manufacturers in India or China to be put into production. Using these systems means that the work is done much more efficiently than if we had to make any changes on paper pattern pieces and send it by post to the manufacturers – the whole process is very quick using CAD/CAM.

WHAT'S THE MOST CHALLENGING ASPECT OF YOUR ROLE?

The whole job is a challenge! When you first get given something new to work on you have to figure out the best way of interpreting the designer's ideas, and find solutions to often complex designs. Although it's challenging, it's in a good way – it makes the job interesting.

IS PATTERN CUTTING AN EXCITING CAREER CHOICE?

Absolutely. I think it's really exciting to be able to create a new product from scratch. Pattern cutting doesn't have the same glamour factor as design

(people perceive the design sector as glamorous but not necessarily the pattern-cutting side). However, there are so many people out there who want to be designers – literally thousands of people looking for work – that my advice is to do a bit of both if possible. If you want to be a designer, make sure that you have a solid training in the pattern-cutting side too – you will be much more employable if you have a really good understanding of how garments go together and are able to execute your ideas well rather than just sketching pretty pictures on paper.

If you have a solid foundation in pattern cutting from the start, you will have another career choice to go back to if you decide that design isn't for you. Also,

it's extremely satisfying and exciting to be able to produce something from nothing – I get a real buzz from design, but to be able to make a garment is even better than just having a sketch.

HOW MUCH TRAVEL IS INVOLVED IN THIS TYPE OF ROLE? It depends on the company you work for, but most pattern cutters are studio-based. A few people in my team have been sent overseas to oversee work in the factories and make sure our product is as good as possible.

Because of my experience of liaising with manufacturers in India with Monsoon, I may get the opportunity to go on trips there in the future.

Photo of a Pattern Cutter (note - this is an example, and is not Ann Watson nor related to AllSaints) Image: CandyBoxPhoto/Shutterstock Images LLC

Our panel of production experts includes Paul Corben, June Lawrence and Ann Watson, who all have extensive industry experience (read their interviews on the previous pages to find out how they began their careers). Here they've answered your questions on getting into product development, pattern cutting and garment technology.

WHAT EXACTLY IS PRODUCT DEVELOPMENT?

There are two distinct types in my opinion. One is taking design briefs and then liaising with factories to ensure samples are the correct specifications and following through to order stage. The other is more creative, taking initial ideas and working with factories, designers and pattern cutters to obtain a distinctive new product.

PAUL CORBEN

IS PATTERN CUTTING CREATIVE OR NOT?

Yes, it can be very creative but this depends on what type of product you specialise in, and the type of company you are working for. In my current role, it's very creative because the product is detailed and interesting. The role is very hands-on and, if you're an experienced pattern cutter, you can often make suggestions to make the product even better than the designer's original sketch, which is really satisfying.

ANN WATSON

IS GARMENT TECHNOLOGY AN EXCITING CAREER CHOICE?

I wouldn't say it's an exciting career choice in that it doesn't come with any of the kudos or acclaim that a designer gets. However, if you wish to be stimulated and challenged daily, provide a real, but sometimes misunderstood service, then being a garment technologist is a good career choice. So many areas are covered by this umbrella title, and what is particularly nice is that it is constantly evolving and changing, so your skill can be updated too, which is always good when thinking of career advancement.

JUNE LAWRENCE

WHAT WOULD I TAKE TO A PRODUCT DEVELOPMENT JOB INTERVIEW? WOULD I NEED A PORTFOLIO OF WORK/EVIDENCE OF GARMENTS I'VE WORKED ON?

It's always good to have examples of any previous work or product you have developed. For instance, you might have created a garment, piece of jewellery or an accessory at home. It's good for the interviewer to see what you are able to do, and for you to be able to explain why you made certain decisions –

e.g. the type of fastening you used, type of fabric or trim, etc. You could also take new ideas mood boards, including information on colour palette, trim, materials, shape and so on.

PAUL CORBEN

IS PRODUCT DEVELOPMENT QUITE REPETITIVE?

Never! No two hours, let alone days, are the same. Things change so quickly that you always have to be alert and proactive.

PAUL CORBEN

IS THIS SECTOR MORE SCIENCE-BASED THAN CREATIVE?

I would say that it is a marriage of the two, as I wouldn't be able to do the technical side without having studied fashion and design. I use Excel formulas and grading increments to grade the different sizes, so you have a well-fitting garment. We also use testing laboratories to carry out testing of the fabrics to establish such things as colour fastness for washing and whether the fabric is likely to shrink or not, so you are never disappointed with your selected garment. Science is a tool and creativity is the end result.

JUNE LAWRENCE

DO MOST PRODUCT DEVELOPERS WORK AT A PARTICULAR MARKET LEVEL, E.G. IN LUXURY STUDIOS? OR IS IT EASY TO WORK AT MANY MARKET LEVELS, E.G. HIGH STREET, BRANDED, ETC?

Most people specialise in one particular area, as it can be difficult to swap between product areas and levels. For instance, the luxury sector can be hard to break into unless you began your career at this market level.

PAUL CORBEN

IS THIS A COMPETITIVE SECTOR OF THE INDUSTRY TO GET INTO?

Yes it is, more so than it used to be, but less so than design. You are still likely to find a job in the production/technical sector more quickly than in the design sector.

ANN WATSON

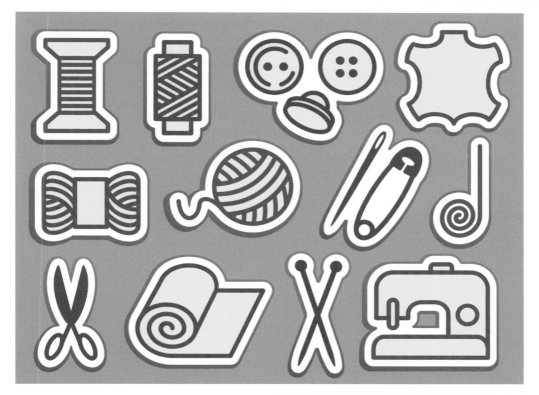

Yes, I would say so because, although it is sometimes a misunderstood area, it plays a vital role in the fashion industry, dealing as it does with fit, fabric and production issues. It has a reasonable salary too.
JUNE LAWRENCE

WHAT CAN YOUNG PEOPLE WHO ARE STILL AT SCHOOL DO TO PREPARE THEMSELVES FOR THIS CAREER ROUTE?

Be inquisitive – when on work experience ask as many questions as you can in order to find out how things are made.
PAUL CORBEN

A love for fashion and clothes is a must, and an inquisitive nature. I loved sewing and making things when I was in my teens. I think that any young people who are interested in this career must be aware of garment construction, understand the behaviour of different fabrics, and have an appreciation of how clothes fit different body shapes.
JUNE LAWRENCE

Image: Katsiaryna/Shutterstock Images LLC

WHAT IS THE INTERVIEW PROCESS FOR THE GARMENT TECHNOLOGIST ROLE – WOULD IT BE TEST-BASED, AND HOW WOULD THE EMPLOYER EXPECT YOU TO PREPARE?

Some companies have a written paper, which is scored, with questions such as what the different wash-care symbols mean, and some have a garment with several faults for you to list, along with suggestions of how to rectify them. You could get either one or both of these accompanying a tough interview to test your knowledge. Some have been known to last for around three hours. An employer would expect you to have researched the company, as is usual, and, if it is a brand, to have checked out their garments in store and prepared a list of what you liked and didn't like about them, and a list of areas where you could perhaps make improvements.
JUNE LAWRENCE

DO MOST PEOPLE IN THIS SECTOR HAVE A DEGREE?

Yes, most have a degree. For older people in this sector, their knowledge and experience play a big part and is the equivalent of a degree in some cases. However, universities now have great courses that

cover all aspects of the industry and give a good foundation for all students.
JUNE LAWRENCE

WHAT WOULD I TAKE TO A PATTERN CUTTING JOB INTERVIEW?

If you're going for an entry-level role, the employer wouldn't expect you to take a huge amount – enthusiasm for the job is more important. However, it would help if you could take along some photographs of garments you have made (with examples of the development process, such as pattern pieces on the mannequin) and some sketches to show your design ideas.
ANN WATSON

WHAT ARE THE BEST THINGS ABOUT WORKING IN GARMENT TECHNOLOGY?

One of the best things is the team I work with. They are very creative and experienced and, despite our occasional differences, they are brilliant. Another good thing is the product area. Menswear is exciting and, despite our restraints and limitations with fabric and costs, I am always impressed by how good our collections are when the salesman samples come in – I sometimes have to remind myself that it belongs to our brand!
JUNE LAWRENCE

WHAT ARE THE THREE WORST THINGS ABOUT WORKING IN GARMENT TECHNOLOGY?

Number one is easy, and that's measuring the garments. It is tedious and slow but a really important part of the job, as it ensures our measurements are being accurately followed by the factories.

The second is dealing with the more unusual sizes, such as working on product for guys who are 6 ft 9 in! The grading for these guys is irregular, and requires a lot of concentration, also finding a fit model is challenging but thankfully not impossible.

The third worst is the erratic work flow. Sometimes I end up working late – I'm so incredibly busy I'm in danger of bumping into myself, because I'm rushing around so quickly. Then other times it's much quieter, and I have more time and the luxury to answer my e-mails straight away without any delay.
JUNE LAWRENCE

IN PATTERN CUTTING, DO MOST PEOPLE STILL WORK BY HAND/ON THE STAND, OR DO MOST COMPANIES WANT PEOPLE TO HAVE EXPERIENCE ON SPECIALIST PROGRAMS SUCH AS GERBER?

Lots of people do still work by hand – but in future I would say that the majority of companies will need staff to be trained in digital pattern cutting on one of the computer programs, such as Gerber or Lectra. If you have skills in those programs, you will be much more employable, so try to choose a course or university where you will get the opportunity to learn the basics.

Even though I have years of experience on manual cutting, I'm in the process of taking night classes in Gerber – it will definitely be a bonus in order to compete for roles in future.
ANN WATSON

To Do List

▶ **PRACTISE** your pattern-cutting and sewing skills — the earlier the better. Having these skills will be a huge advantage when it comes to finding work experience or when you start a fashion course at college or university. Buy a pattern from a haberdashery shop or department store (stores like John Lewis have a good selection), get yourself some cheap fabric and, if you don't have one already, try to borrow a sewing machine or buy a cheap second-hand one from eBay (or look for them at car boot sales). Basic new models can be bought relatively cheaply for approximately £50 from John Lewis.

▶ **STUDY** how garments and accessories are made. This can be as simple as looking at different products when you're out shopping — take note of the types of fabric used and the differences between materials, what heels are made from on shoes and how they're constructed, the type of fastenings and trims used on a bag or purse. Start a notebook of all the things that catch your eye and begin to think about how certain products could be improved or changed — question everything and think about why an item has been made in a certain way. Jot down what you think is interesting, innovative, clever — take your notebook everywhere so you can document as much as possible when you're out and about.

▶ **DECONSTRUCT** old clothes and accessories to see how they're made — then develop something new from them. If you have anything you don't wear anymore, think about how you could improve or change it — cut bits off, add things on, make it into a completely new garment. Ann Watson explains: "When I was still at school I used to buy cheap things from charity shops to cut up, dye and attach new details — the satisfaction of creating something new to wear is huge, and it's totally unique."

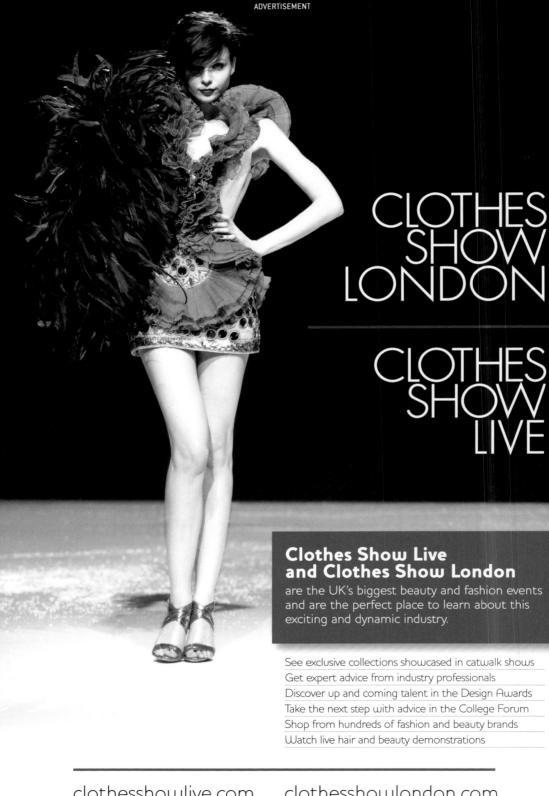

CLOTHES
SHOW
LONDON

CLOTHES
SHOW
LIVE

**Clothes Show Live
and Clothes Show London**
are the UK's biggest beauty and fashion events
and are the perfect place to learn about this
exciting and dynamic industry.

See exclusive collections showcased in catwalk shows
Get expert advice from industry professionals
Discover up and coming talent in the Design Awards
Take the next step with advice in the College Forum
Shop from hundreds of fashion and beauty brands
Watch live hair and beauty demonstrations

clothesshowlive.com   clothesshowlondon.com

Photographer: Chris Moore / Show production: John Walford

IN THIS CHAPTER:

Show Production: Luke Foy / Photographer: Christopher Dadey

"You need to know about different cultural and creative industries – it's not all about what's happening in fashion."

John Walford, Show Producer

WHAT DOES A FASHION SHOW PRODUCER DO?

The role of a show producer carries a lot of responsibility as it involves creating a certain look or theme for a client (usually a fashion designer) and the ability to generate a team to execute that idea as effectively as possible. This will include working closely with the designer or client to develop the theme or look for the show (also often working on the creative element in collaboration with an appointed fashion stylist). The theme is central to the success of the event, and must showcase the style and talent of the designer in the best possible light.

The style of each show can vary hugely, depending on the budget, type of clothing being used, and the signature of the designer or brand. Some shows can be huge, flamboyant and conceptual events, with special effects and complicated choreography, while others will be much simpler. Apart from having a huge role in the creative aspects of the show, the producer and their team are the ones who make sure that all the technical elements are correct, and that, ultimately, everyone is in the right place at the right time so the show runs smoothly. They will need to co-ordinate a huge team of people, and should be able to remain calm under pressure, and juggle many different responsibilities at once.

WHO EMPLOYS FASHION SHOW PRODUCERS?

Experienced show producers are mainly self-employed and have their own production companies. People new to the industry usually work freelance; because the work is project-based and they are not needed all the time, the majority of assistants aren't full-time employees. The majority of projects occur during the annual Fashion Weeks, with most during February/March and September/October.

The main production companies are based in major fashion capitals, such as London, New York, Paris and Milan. Their clients include established fashion designers (for one-off, couture and ready-to-wear shows), retailers, brands, fashion colleges/universities and event management companies.

KEY WORKING RELATIONSHIPS

The role of a show producer is to establish a 'dream team' of people to make the show as successful as possible. Over the years, they will develop strong working relationships with people they know and trust, who they can rely on to help deliver a great event.

On a day-to-day basis, the producer will be responsible for a team of assistants, and will also liaise with an extensive list of fashion professionals, including model agents, PR agencies and event managers. On the day of a show, the producer will be expected to co-ordinate the models, make-up artists, hair stylists, fashion stylists, and DJs, as well as a team of dressers, set builders, lighting designers and sound engineers.

All this on top of keeping their main client – more often than not a highly stressed and tired designer or creative director – as happy and calm as possible. It's definitely not a job for the faint-hearted or easily stressed!

RELATED ROLES

People who have worked in show production may often cross over into other sectors, including event management, theatre and set design, music and lighting design, styling and visual merchandising.

WORKING HOURS

Working in show production can be very tiring in the run-up to and during the actual event. There are rarely set hours to work to – staff will be expected to work for as long as it takes to get the job done, often under extreme pressure. This isn't a 9–5 role, and work can be at night, weekends and over holidays.

SALARY

As with the majority of roles in fashion that are seen as the most glamorous, jobs in show production don't tend to pay highly until you reach a certain level of seniority, or have a good track record.

People starting out might work for free on a few shows to get their name out there and gain some relevant experience and contacts, gradually building up to about £15k per year. It's difficult to give an average salary for this sector, as the amounts paid per show can vary so much. Show producers tend to be paid a set fee per project by their client, rather than a day rate.

EDUCATION:

Useful school subjects: Art & Design, Music, Drama/Theatre Studies, Languages, Textiles
There aren't any specialist courses on fashion show production; most assistants come from either general fashion design courses, or have studied fashion marketing, promotion or communication at degree level. Many graduates also come from courses focused on the theatre, TV, film or event management. The show producers we spoke to explained that practical work experience on a CV is more important than a qualification.

BEST THINGS ABOUT THE JOB

My work has taken me to some wonderful places and I've met really inspiring and interesting people, many of whom have become great friends. I also love the fact that no two days are ever the same — I can't stand the drudgery of a 9–5 work day.
LUKE FOY, SHOW PRODUCER

It can be very exciting when an idea one has had turns out not only to work but also to be very successful.
JOHN WALFORD, SHOW PRODUCER/CO-FOUNDER OF VAUXHALL FASHION SCOUT

WORST THINGS ABOUT THE JOB

It can be frustrating just how unadventurous and boring some clients are.
JOHN WALFORD

Early call times, cancelled models, and never quite knowing where the next job will come from.
LUKE FOY

Show Production: Luke Foy/Photographer: Chris Moore

WHAT SKILLS ARE NEEDED TO WORK IN FASHION SHOW PRODUCTION?

- You need to be extremely organised and efficient, flexible and able to work well under pressure
- Above all you must have good people skills. You will be expected to deal with all sorts of difficult and high-maintenance people in this job, and have the capacity to organise a team quickly and effectively
- Creativity and being able to 'think outside the box' is essential
- Excellent technical skills are a must — you should have a good working knowledge of the lighting and sound elements of the job, and be able to establish quickly what is or isn't possible. There's no point having an amazing creative idea, but not being able to execute it
- Being able to speak another language can come in very useful, especially Mandarin, Cantonese, French and Italian

Luke is a self-employed Show Producer based in London. He works with a variety of clients, including fashion designers, A Child of the Jago and Bora Aksu. In between fashion weeks he also works on shows at music festivals across the UK. You can see his work at www.lukefoy.com

Industry Insider!

EDUCATION
School: Maths, Sciences, English, Art, History, Spanish and German
College: A-levels in Art, History and Psychology followed by an Art Foundation course
University: Luke studied at Nottingham Trent University and completed two years of a Fashion Design course before transferring to International Fashion Business.

WHAT MADE YOU GO INTO SHOW PRODUCTION?
I quickly learned that the creative process I enjoyed the most was producing the end-of-semester shows at college rather than sewing, which I was terrible at!

DID YOU DO WORK EXPERIENCE WHEN YOU STARTED OUT? Yes, my first role was with the annual Graduate Fashion Week (GFW) in London, initially assisting on site during the event week.

HOW DID YOU GET YOUR FIRST JOB IN SHOW PRODUCTION? I had the good fortune to meet John Walford, one of the co-founders of both Graduate Fashion Week and Vauxhall Fashion Scout, while interning at GFW and somehow talked my way into assisting him. I did this for around four years before starting to produce shows in my own right. John and I continue to be great friends and we also work together occasionally.

IS THIS CAREER AS YOU EXPECTED IT TO BE BEFORE YOU STARTED OUT? To be honest I didn't really have any expectations — the unpredictability of the business is something that I love.

THIS INDUSTRY IS OFTEN SEEN AS QUITE GLAMOROUS — WOULD YOU AGREE OR DISAGREE? On the face of it show production may appear glamorous, but early starts, long days and the fact that my phone never stops ringing during Fashion Week can make for a somewhat stressful reality. I'm generally too tired to stay very long at any of the parties either! Being self-employed can also be very difficult at times, without the security of a regular salary.

DO YOU EVER FEEL NERVOUS ABOUT BEING RESPONSIBLE FOR SUCH BIG SHOWS? I'd be lying if I said no. Pre-show there's always a strange combination of excitement and nerves but I have a great team that works with me, so there really is no need to be nervous.

HOW LONG DOES IT TAKE TO ORGANISE A SHOW?
It depends on the event. I like to be involved with my designers throughout the design process — knowing what their inspiration is helps with my part of the job. I generally have a few meetings in the weeks before the show to discuss ideas for music, lighting and choreography. We start casting and placing options on models around a week before the show. On show day I normally arrive four hours before it starts, as do the models and the rest of the backstage team. The models go straight into hair and make-up and the time disappears with preparations — sound and lighting checks, rehearsals and last-minute fittings.

WHAT'S THE MOST DIFFICULT DECISION YOU'VE HAD TO MAKE IN YOUR CAREER? Persevering at being freelance when times were tough and when lots of friends from uni were getting good jobs.

WHEN THE SHOW RUNS SMOOTHLY, HOW DO YOU FEEL? Proud and happy for my clients, and also excited to see the photos in the press or online.

WHAT ADVICE WOULD YOU GIVE TO SOMEONE JUST STARTING OUT? Fashion is a small world where everyone knows each other — there are so many people at the shows, you never know who you are talking to backstage and you never know who may employ you next. So it's important to work hard, be on time, be nice to everyone and try to get involved with organising events and shows at college.

Luke in HUGE glasses!

Portrait of Luke Foy / Photographer: Will Sanders

Show Production: John Walford, Show Assistant: Luke Foy/Photographer: Chris Moore

Show production is often viewed as one of the more glamorous jobs in fashion — but is it really like that, and what can you do to prepare for this career route? We've put some questions on show production to one of the leading show producers in London.

John Walford: John has an impressive CV in show production. Co-founder of Graduate Fashion Week, he has been at the forefront of fashion for many years, and has worked on shows for a huge variety of high-profile designers, including Vivienne Westwood, Hussein Chalayan and Ashish. Based in London (but often working overseas), he is co-founder of Vauxhall Fashion Scout (www.vauxhallfashionscout.com), as well as being the Director of Shanghai Fashion Week.

WHAT DOES AN AVERAGE DAY INVOLVE?

On the day of a show, it involves working to a time line (establishing when the models arrive, when the dressers arrive, scheduling and overseeing the rehearsal) and making sure everyone is aware of the times and making everything happen like clockwork. Organisation and being able to cope under pressure are essential. For instance, if a model is late, you should know how to react because you know what you are doing and can come up with a back-up plan.

IS THIS A DIFFICULT SECTOR OF THE INDUSTRY TO GET INTO?

I think it is quite easy to get into on a very superficial level, like helping a friend who is a designer. To earn a living out of it is much harder, as the trust required to be given the amount of control that a producer has takes a lot of time and effort to establish. There

is also much more competition out there in the sector than there used to be, with approximately 12 established fashion show production companies competing for the same business. This, combined with the fact that clients have much less money to spend than they used to a few years ago, makes it a difficult industry for many to earn a decent living from — only a few show producers have this as their main source of income.

WHAT OPPORTUNITIES EXIST FOR PEOPLE WANTING TO GET INTO THIS SECTOR?

There are many opportunities in theory but I have found that very few people have wanted to stick at it once they realise how much work is involved and how difficult the client can be. Also, work can be erratic — one minute we have loads of work, other times can be much quieter — so anyone looking for

All images — John Walford

a job in show production must be prepared for a lack of career stability and be able to cope with that.

WHAT QUALIFICATIONS ARE NEEDED TO GET INTO THIS SECTOR – IS A DEGREE ESSENTIAL?

I do not think a degree is essential. Not all the show producers have one (but one has to say we are generally slightly older), but I have a degree in Drama and Theatre Arts.

HOW CAN STUDENTS PREPARE FOR A CAREER IN SHOW PRODUCTION – WHAT CAN THEY BE DOING WHILE STILL AT SCHOOL OR COLLEGE TO ENHANCE THEIR SKILLS?

I worked in the theatre – stage management and directing – which gave me a great foundation for the skills needed in fashion show production. I would recommend that students gain some work experience at their local theatre, but the most important thing is to be taught good habits (being on time, being able to pass on information) as well as specific practical skills.

WHAT ARE YOUR TOP TIPS FOR ASPIRING SHOW PRODUCERS?

Go to the theatre, watch ballet, go to exhibitions and keep yourself stimulated and informed. Working in fashion show production, you will need to know about many different cultural and creative industries – it's not all about what's happening in fashion alone.

WHICH COURSES WOULD YOU RECOMMEND FOR SOMEONE WHO WANTS TO GET INTO THIS SECTOR? IN FACT ARE THERE ANY COURSES FOCUSING ON THIS SECTOR?

To the best of my knowledge there are no specialist courses for fashion show production. The majority of people in this industry have come from a more general fashion course, or another sector such as theatre production.

WHAT WOULD IMPRESS YOU IN SOMEONE LOOKING FOR WORK EXPERIENCE?

Enthusiasm. It is amazing how many people lose interest in the job when they discover how mundane much of the work is and how much time is spent waiting around for the main event to happen (during which time they have to stay alert and focused, always ready to help out when required).

To Do List

▶ **GAIN** some hands-on work experience. There's nothing better than experiencing the job to see if it's really for you or not. Not everyone lives in a location where there are top catwalk shows, but that doesn't matter. What's more important is that you work somewhere where you can pick up practical knowledge of the job and take on some proper responsibility, rather than getting a big name on your CV (although it's great if you can secure work at a major event or show, it's not essential). If you're at school or college, take the initiative and offer to stage a fashion show, using clothes students have made, or from local designers, stores or even charity stores – what better way to gain experience than being completely responsible for the event?

Look out for fashion shows, galas and charity events in your area by checking your local newspaper or community magazine – most event organisers will welcome an extra pair of hands to help out. Also contact your nearest fashion college or university as they may need assistance when they hold fashion shows for the graduating students.

You can also gain experience working as a dresser at fashion shows. There are specialist dressing agencies, whose job it is to provide staff to assist the models get ready backstage. They're always looking out for extra people, especially during fashion weeks.

Getting work experience somewhere like a theatre will also help to strengthen your technical skills and your understanding of how lighting, set and sound design work. As John Walford mentioned earlier in this chapter, these are invaluable skills to have and will set you apart from most other applicants out there.

▶ **WATCH** fashion shows online so you can see the different techniques used in the staging of a show. Make notes on what you like, what you don't like, what inspires you and why. You can see shows by looking at websites such as **www.style.com** (where you can watch videos and hear the music too) and **www.firstview.com**

When I did the market research for this book, most of the people who completed my survey about what concerns them about a career in fashion listed 'finding work experience' at the top. As all the industry insiders have stressed throughout each chapter, getting work experience is key to your future success in the industry, so I've tried to answer as many of your questions about it as possible over the next few pages. Happy job-hunting, and good luck!

I'M SEARCHING FOR WORK EXPERIENCE BUT CAN'T SEEM TO FIND ANYTHING – WHERE CAN I LOOK?

Not all roles are advertised, so you will have to do a lot of research to find the most suitable ones for you. Many companies find work experience students via word-of-mouth recommendations through their own contacts, or by responding to people who have sent their details to the company directly, so there's often no need for them to advertise. The people who are successful in finding work experience are those who use a couple of different methods and who are very proactive in their search. Here's how you can increase your chances of finding something:

▶ APPLY DIRECTLY

If you already have an idea of the companies you want to work for, it's best to make a list of them on a spreadsheet and begin to apply on a speculative basis (i.e. send your details to them even if a role hasn't been advertised). There's a certain amount of luck involved in this method – it's all about you being in the right place at the right time (or your CV being in the right place at the right time). It sounds obvious, but the more CVs you send out, the higher the chance of you finding something.

Many people get frustrated and down at the lack of response when they've only sent their details to some ten companies. Remember that you might need to send your CV to at least 50–100 companies before being successful, so try to remain focused and positive about the process. The people who win in the end are the ones who don't give up at the first hurdle. You have to remain persistent and work hard at finding a placement – it won't happen overnight.

▶ ASK YOUR SCHOOL/COLLEGE OR UNIVERSITY FOR HELP

Most careers advisers, teachers and tutors at your school/college/university should have contacts within the industry, so follow up any leads they have given you. Don't dismiss recommendations if they don't automatically appeal or aren't exactly what you had in mind – it's very rare to get the 'perfect' work placement, especially if you're still at high school or in the sixth form. Remember that you will still learn a lot – about punctuality, time management, etc – and gain more confidence, whatever type of placement you do.

▶ LOOK IN LOCAL MAGAZINES/NEWSPAPERS

Take a look in the job section of your local paper or community magazine for businesses who are advertising for staff – a great opportunity might be right on your doorstep!

▶ USE YOUR CONTACTS

It's surprising how many people don't use the contacts they already have. Of course, not everyone knows people within the industry, but try to think of someone who might be useful to you: a friend of a friend who already works in the business, a school/college tutor who used to work in fashion, your cousin who's already done a work placement (they might be able to pass on some useful names), your mum's friend who's a designer, and so on. All these people – or others you can think of – could help you find a placement, but it's up to you to let them know that you're looking for something – there's no point being shy about it. I once spoke to a student whose mum was friends with the head of design at a major fashion brand, but the student hadn't contacted him for fear of being thought pushy! What a wasted opportunity. Don't be afraid to ask for help – this business is all about self-promotion and being confident. Also, most people are only too happy to help – after all, they were once in the same position as you.

▶ CHECK ONLINE

As mentioned above, not all companies advertise their work experience vacancies, but luckily there are a few that use online advertising/networking to find staff.

Here are a co
work experie

www.fashior
This is an an
work placem
and feature:
accessories design, illustration, styling, make up,
journalism, PR and marketing, event management,
admin and pattern cutting. Another great facility
on this site is that you can advertise the fact that
you're looking for work — for free. The site is used by
employers who are looking for interns, so you might
just get spotted and asked in for an interview. Make
sure your information is written in a professional
manner, and double check for spelling mistakes
before posting.

www.gorkanapr.com
Look in the Interns section to find roles in fashion PR
and fashion journalism — there are some fantastic
opportunities listed here with really well-known
publications.

www.fashioncapital.co.uk
Various internships are listed in the Jobs Forum
section of this extensive website.

www.nineteen74.com
This is a fashion networking site, and attracts people
from all over the world. There are internships listed in
the Jobs section, with the majority of roles focused
on fashion journalism/blogging. As it's a networking
site, you can also create a profile here. If you're
looking for a creative role, you can upload designs or
photos from your portfolio to showcase your talent to
prospective employers.

www.fashionunited.co.uk
This site is a great place to find out up-to-date
information and news about what's happening in
the fashion industry. Take a look in the Internships in
Fashion section (in the Jobs page) — there are often
overseas roles as well as UK-based positions.

www.gumtree.com
There aren't lots of fashion postings here, but it's
worth a look — you never know what you might find.

FERENCE BETWEEN AN INTERNSHIP, NCE AND WORK PLACEMENT?

ially mean the same thing. Strictly
iternship used to mean just unpaid
:e and is the term used in the US for
irk. Some companies use the term
lescribe any type of work experience,
hecking with each one before taking
up any offer of employment to confirm whether it's a
paid or unpaid position.

DOES IT MATTER THAT MY WORK EXPERIENCE IN SIXTH FORM DIDN'T INVOLVE FASHION?

If you've already done your 'official' work experience
at school or college and it didn't involve fashion,
don't worry too much. You will still have (it's hoped!)
learned important skills in time management and
become more confident during your placement.
Also, there's still the opportunity to do extra work
experience during the school holidays and during
further/higher education.

HOW LONG ARE COMPANIES WILLING TO TAKE YOU ON IN THE HOLIDAYS? IS ONLY A WEEK OR TWO ENOUGH?

Any experience is useful — if the company can only
take you for a week or two, that's alright. However,
you might find that lots of companies actually prefer
to take people for longer periods of time — most need
an 'extra pair of hands' to help out, and it's easier
for them to arrange to have one person in for three
or four weeks, rather than having to co-ordinate and
train several different people for shorter periods.
Having a longer work placement is more beneficial
for you too, as it allows you to learn more about how
the company works, gain increased responsibility,
and make a lasting impression.

WHY ARE THERE ONLY OPPORTUNITIES IN LONDON AND NOT THE SURROUNDING AREAS?

While it's true that most roles are in London (and
other fashion capitals, such as Paris, Milan, New
York, etc) because most major fashion companies
have their head offices based there (for ease of
accessibility, prestige of having their office in a
capital city, etc), opportunities do exist throughout
other areas. In the UK, some companies have bases
in the Midlands and North West (such as Next,
George at Asda and Per Una), and the South East, and
there are a few in Scotland (textile companies and
mills). If you've set your sights on working only for
a major brand or retailer, it's likely that you'll have

to travel to get to your placement. However, don't dismiss working for a smaller, local business. For instance, if it's design you want to get into, most towns or cities will have independent designers who have their own studios. These won't be 'big name' designers, but people who design and make made-to-measure garments for private clients, especially wedding dresses or party/occasionwear.

Working for a company like this will give you the opportunity to be much more 'hands-on' than if working for a large corporate company, as you're likely to be working directly with the owner of the company and seeing exactly what is involved in every aspect of the business.

WHY CAN'T THE INDUSTRY TAKE STUDENTS WHO ARE STILL AT SCHOOL MORE SERIOUSLY WHEN IT COMES TO WORK EXPERIENCE? I'M BEING TURNED DOWN AS COMPANIES SAY THEY WANT SOMEONE OLDER.

Getting into the industry is so competitive that you will be up against many other students (and even graduates who have already left university) for a limited number of work placements. Most companies are more likely to take on students who are already a couple of years into further or higher education and who are studying on fashion courses. They know these students will have gained specialist skills at college or uni, such as in computer programs, sewing, pattern cutting, etc, and have learned the correct terminology relating to their particular sector.

As employers usually want people with a certain amount of confidence and maturity who they can rely upon to 'hit the ground running' (i.e. someone who can fit into the business with a minimal amount of training), they are more likely to go for college or university students rather than those still at school when it comes to recruitment for work experience.

This isn't always the case (there are always companies out there willing to give someone the opportunity), but it may take you a little longer than expected to find something, so start making applications long before you need to get a placement.

DO YOU GET PAID FOR DOING WORK EXPERIENCE?

The vast majority of people on work experience don't get paid, especially if they're still at school or college rather than university. It's quite common to receive

...money, and sometimes free clothes or products, but don't expect it – be prepared to have to fund yourself throughout work experience.

Students who are completing work placements as part of a university course sometimes get paid if they are employed for between six months and a year, but this is relatively uncommon, and is more usual with a large corporate company rather than a small private business.

HOW DO PEOPLE AFFORD TO DO FULL-TIME INTERNSHIPS/WORK PLACEMENTS? IS THERE ANY FUNDING FOR STUDENTS?

Doing an internship/work experience can be expensive, especially if you have to move away from home to complete it. If you haven't already got a part-time job, now is the time to get one, so you can begin to save. Once on work placement, some students have another part-time job alongside, such as bar or retail work. This option isn't for everyone though, and you will have to decide whether you can cope with the extra workload – you don't want to end up being too tired to cope on your work placement.

Unfortunately, there are very limited options when it comes to funding. One organisation that might be able to help is the Prince's Trust, which offers financial assistance for travel to and from work placements. Visit its website at:
www.princes-trust.org.uk

WHAT ANNOYS EMPLOYERS AND WHAT IMPRESSES THEM?

The answer to this question could take a few pages, but here's a brief summary:

IMPRESS:

▶ Genuine enthusiasm for the job/company

▶ When the applicant has really done their research on the company before applying/being interviewed

▶ Politeness – be courteous when applying for roles. In your covering letter you shouldn't be sloppy, over-familiar or arrogant

▶ Strong presentation – your CV, covering letter and interview technique should be spot on. There are no excuses for poor spelling in your written application or for being under-prepared for an interview

▶ Someone who has taken the time to prepare additional material when they apply or are interviewed for a job – take a look at the answer to the question below for more info on how to stand out from the crowd

▶ Once on work experience, the people who impress employers are the ones who go that extra mile (and, as mentioned previously, don't complain about the duller jobs). Punctuality and good attendance will also get you noticed – no employer will be impressed by someone who constantly turns up late (with a different excuse each time) or who's always taking time off.

ANNOY:

▶ Employers can spot a generic covering letter a mile off (i.e. when someone uses the same letter to send to *every* company they apply to). While it's fine to use a template as the basis of your letter, you should adjust it slightly each time to make it a bit more personal. Even worse is when a company receives a letter from someone who hasn't even bothered to check what the company *does*. (I've received letters from people asking for work experience who say they want to use their skills in my design studio. I don't have a design studio.)

▶ Text speak – don't use it in your covering letter! Always keep any correspondence professional – it's better to be slightly too formal than too informal. When applying via email remember to use the same rules as you would when writing a letter.

▶ Unprofessional e-mail addresses are a no-no! As the majority of job applications are done via e-mail, it's important to consider how you will come across to an employer – for instance, an address such as sexyxxpinkprincess@hotmail.com or dozygirlinlalaland@gmail.com is unlikely to impress anyone. If you have a personal e-mail that could be misinterpreted, it's worth setting up a new one just for your job applications. First name with last name and a number is a good, safe option.

▶ Calling the company every day after you've sent your application doesn't endear you to prospective bosses. While it's good to be persistent,

don't go over the top and harass the company you want to work for. Wait at least three or four days after sending your information before calling or e-mailing to see if they're interested. (Monday mornings aren't the best time to call, as most employers will be catching up on e-mails after the weekend or having their weekly meetings. Friday afternoons are generally better, when people might be less stressed.)

If you've left two or three messages and sent e-mails without receiving a response, it's generally safe to say that you haven't been successful. However, some companies do keep details of applicants on file for future reference, so you might be surprised with a call a few weeks or even months later.

HOW CAN I STAND OUT FROM THE CROWD WHEN SENDING MY APPLICATION – SURELY COMPANIES GET INUNDATED WITH CVS?

Most employers receive hundreds more CVs for each role than they actually need, but there is something you can do to try to stand out from everyone else applying. This involves sending something extra in addition to your CV and covering letter to show the company you've done your research on them and you understand what they do, and demonstrate the skills you can offer.

So, if you're going for a design role, you can put together a trend/theme page plus a few pages of designs done in their style. (Do your figure illustrations to look like their customer – if you've done some research by going into their stores or looking on their website, you should have an idea of who their core customer is. This includes what sort of hairstyle they have, the shoes they wear, and their accessories and make-up). Send some colour photocopies or attach the images as jpg or pdf files if applying by e-mail.

Or if you're interested in working as a fashion journalist, prospective employers will want to see how you write, and if your style is suitable for them. Put together a mock article in the style of the publication you want to work for – this could be a fashion feature, a trend report, or anything you feel would be suitable for them.

The same can be applied to any other sector – think about what would be suitable for the area of fashion you want to work in. For instance, a trend board would be good to send to a trend forecasting agency, a mock press release to a PR agency, etc.

Whatever you create, focus on quality, not quantity. If you've taken the time to put a special project together for a company, you're much more likely to get called in for an interview as you will have shown much more enthusiasm, commitment and initiative than someone who's just sent a copy of their CV.

WHAT WOULD I EXPECT TO DO ON A PLACEMENT, PRE-DEGREE?

Duties vary greatly depending on the company you go to and sector you work in – everywhere is different. However, generally speaking, most students will be expected to carry out general admin tasks, such as filing, answering the phone, data input, research, photocopying, and all of the other random small jobs which crop up in a busy fashion office or studio. While this doesn't sound like the most exciting thing in the world, approach any task you're given with enthusiasm, and make sure you do every job well (even if it's making the MD's coffee – hang on, *especially* if it's making the MD's coffee!). If it's noticed that you are doing these seemingly small things well, you're likely to be trusted with more responsibility and more interesting tasks as the placement progresses.

WHAT ARE THE CHANCES OF INTERNSHIPS LEADING TO FULL-TIME PAID POSITIONS?

If you impress your employers while on work experience, there's every chance they'll take you back once you're ready for full-time employment. In fact, this is one of the best ways of finding a role on graduation from university or college – many graduates find their first paid job with their work placement company. It's important to keep in contact with the company after you've completed your internship, and to remind them that you're on the look-out for something once you've graduated. Even if they can't offer you paid work, they might be able to recommend you to a company that is looking for someone.

HOW 'ARTY' SHOULD MY CV BE WHEN SENDING OUT TO FASHION COMPANIES?

It's a common misconception that students/graduates applying for art/design-based roles should include pictures or photos, coloured backgrounds,

unusual fonts and so on when doing their CV. You might stand out – but for the wrong reasons. Putting unusual fonts, colours and pictures on a CV can actually detract from the content and the factual text, and simply make the CV more difficult to read.

Most employers only take about 20 seconds to read through a CV, and don't have time to try to make out what you're trying to say. Professional people who already work in the industry don't have gimmicky CVs, so neither should you. In order to demonstrate your creativity and skills, you should be sending additional information with your application (as mentioned above) as separate files or photocopies, rather than trying to pile everything on to your CV. A CV should generally be done in Word format, using an easy-to-read font such as Arial, Times New Roman or Helvetica.

WHAT SHOULD I INCLUDE ON MY CV?

There are many different ways to structure a CV, and the information and layout will change slightly depending on the amount of experience you have and the stage you're at in your education. However, generally speaking, you should structure it as shown opposite.

Use a bold font to highlight the title of each section to make each part more distinctive, and align all text to the left-hand side of the page to make it easier for viewers to skim – it's very hard on the eye if text is placed to the left, in the middle and to the right on the same page.

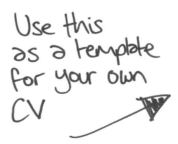

Use this as a template for your own CV

FULL NAME

CONTACT DETAILS
Include an e-mail address, landline phone number and mobile phone number

SUMMARY
A summary of your situation, skills, relevant experience, and what you're looking for, written in bullet point format. This might be similar to the following:

- A-level student – currently in my second year at sixth form college
- Basic skills in computer programs such as Photoshop/Illustrator
- Previous experience of assisting in a fashion studio at ----- *(put company name here)*
- Confident in dealing with customers, due to my experience working in fashion retail
- Looking to contribute my skills within a fast-paced fashion graphic design studio over the summer holidays – available for three weeks during July/August.

EDUCATION
Begin with your most recent situation first, and include a brief overview of the subjects you've studied (you don't need to go into a huge amount of detail about every single module you've done – focus on the subjects/projects you feel will be most relevant in relation to the roles you're applying for). For instance:

2009 – present: Redcliffe Sixth Form College, Redcliffe-on-Sea
Currently studying for A-levels: Art, Textiles, Graphic Design, Media Studies

2004 – 2009: St Mary's High School, Redcliffe-on-Sea
GCSE's: Grades A-B: Art & Design (A*), Textiles, English, IT; Grade C: Maths, Science, History

You don't need to list your primary school

RELEVANT WORK EXPERIENCE
Here you can list any other previous work experience you've done. Try to be as specific as possible regarding the responsibilities you had and what your role involved and list these in bullet point format. Use wording that sounds professional – for instance, "Assisted the womenswear graphic design team within a fast-paced fashion studio, contributing to ideas for their Spring/Summer advertising campaign" rather than "Helped at a fashion company with their designs".

EMPLOYMENT HISTORY
This is different from the section above, as you will list any paid work you have done so far, such as retail, restaurant or bar work. You don't need to list every job you've ever had – just focus on the most recent ones, or roles which demonstrate relevant experience, such as working in fashion companies or if you've gained extra responsibility in a role.

SKILLS
While you may not have many relevant skills yet, do put down anything you feel could contribute to your application. For example:
Basic Photoshop skills: Attended a one-day course at Redcliffe Community College in order to increase my awareness of this specialist computer program. I was given the opportunity to demonstrate these skills during my work placement at ------

ACHIEVEMENTS
Here you can list any additional information you feel might impress employers, eg:

2009 Gained first prize in a design competition run by local newspaper, *The Redcliffe Standard*
Passed driving test at the first attempt

INTERESTS
Most people list very general things in the interests section, such as 'socialising', but try to include things which demonstrate initiative and motivation or goal-oriented interests such as training for a 5k race, raising money for charity, etc.

AVANT-GARDE

Used to describe very conceptual, eccentric or unusual clothing/accessories. Examples of avant-garde designers include Hussein Chalayan and Viktor & Rolf.

BLOCK

In fashion terms, the 'block' is the standard pattern piece a pattern maker or designer will use to develop more complex designs from. They are normally made from cardboard. There will usually be blocks for tops, shirts, trousers, skirts, jackets, dresses and all other types of garment. The designer/pattern maker traces round the block to get a standard shape, and then goes on to create more detailed pattern pieces. In America, the block is called a *sloper*.

CAD/CAM

These abbreviations stand for Computer-Aided Design/Computer-Aided Manufacture, and include specialist programs and packages such as Photoshop, Illustrator and InDesign. These computer systems help designers to design and manufacture products more quickly and efficiently than is possible doing all the work by hand. For instance, when producing a print or graphic design for a garment they are able to test different colourways and patterns at the click of a button.

COUTURE

The French term for exclusive, made-to-measure garments, which are sold to a very small percentage of wealthy clients worldwide.

CRITICAL PATH

This is the timeline/schedule designers and production staff need to follow to ensure that products are created efficiently, on time and with all the correct elements included.

DIFFUSION

Many luxury brands or designer companies produce a cheaper range – a diffusion line – in addition to their more expensive collections, enabling consumers to get their look for less. In America, this is called a *bridge brand*.

E-TAILER

Term used to describe an online store (such as ASOS).

FLAT DRAWING

Sketches drawn by a designer to show exactly where all the detail will go on a garment. These are very precise and clear drawings and are often created on CAD software.

GERBER

Computer software program commonly used in product development and pattern design/grading.

HIGH FASHION

Expensive, luxury items of clothing. Commonly called *haute couture* (French wording), these pieces are made to the highest standards in terms of quality and material.

INTERNSHIP

A period of work placement experience where the employee works for free. More of an American expression, this term is being used more frequently now in the UK.

KEY STYLES

The styles of clothes or accessories chosen each season as 'must-have' items, because of a particular shape, silhouette, colour or pattern.

LINE UP

The final designs that make it into a collection, presented either as finished garments on models, or illustrated figure drawings in a portfolio.

MARKETING MIX

Often known as the '4 Ps', the marketing mix is the process that companies follow when launching a marketing campaign. These are controllable elements, consisting of product, price, promotion and place.

NICHE MARKET

A specialist area of the industry, such as millinery (hat and head-piece design), corporatewear (uniforms, such as for airline staff) or plus-size garments.

OPTITEX

Specialist computer software used to create 3D images of designs, patterns and shapes.

PORTFOLIO

Selection of visual work produced by any creative professional to showcase their skills and best ideas. Most creative people transport and organise their work in an easy-to-carry folder, usually A3 or A4 in size. However, it's becoming more common to display work on a computer or via a portfolio website, which is called a digital portfolio.

RUNWAY

Another name for catwalk at fashion shows.

SHOP REPORT

Information designers and buyers put together, in either visual or written format, in order to research and document what their competitors are doing in terms of product and pricing.

TFP

This stands for 'Test for Portfolio', a common term used mainly by photographers, make-up artists and stylists who collaborate on photo shoots in order to practise their skills and work together as a team, generally when they're in the early stages of their career. TFP images are essential pieces to include in a portfolio for future interviews and work experience.

TOILE

Pronounced 'twall', this is the practice version of a garment once the first pattern has been created, and is used to test how the piece looks and fits before the final version is made in the proper fabric. Depending on the complexity of the garment, a few toiles may be produced before the design and production team are satisfied with the result. Toiles are usually made from a cheap fabric known as calico.

UCAS

Charitable organisation responsible for managing applications to almost all full-time undergraduate degree programmes at UK universities and colleges.

VISUALISATIONS

Realistic and detailed drawings created by textile/graphic designers to demonstrate where their designs would be placed on a garment or accessory.

TOP: Photo of Viki Wittering: Laura Hintz, c/o Lulu Guinness
MIDDLE: Zoran Karapancev/Shutterstock Images LLC
BOTTOM: MUA: Claire Salter / Photographer: James Lightbown

MAGAZINES

Amelia's Magazine
Drapers
Elle
Grazia
Glamour
InStyle
LOOK
Super Super
Vogue

BOOKS

The Look: Adventures in Rock and Pop Fashion
Author: Paul Gorman
2006, Adelita Ltd.

200 Projects to Get You into Fashion Design
Authors: Adrian Grandon & Tracey Fitzgerald
2009, A&C Black Publishers Ltd.

Basics Fashion Design: Construction
Author: Annette Fischer
2008, AVA Publishing

Basics Fashion Design: Fashion Drawing
Author: John Hopkins
2010, AVA Publishing

Fashion Buying
Author: Helen Goworek
2007, John Wiley & Sons

Fashion Forecasting
Authors: Janine Munslow & Kathryn McKelvey
2008, John Wiley & Sons

Fashion Marketing
Author: Mike Easey
2008, John Wiley & Sons

*How Does Your Fashion Show, Show?: How to Present
A Professional Fashion Production*
Author: Barbara Green-Withrow
2008, CreateSpace

Makeup: The Ultimate Guide
Author: Rae Morris
2008, Apple Press

Mastering Fashion Styling (Palgrave Master Series)
Author: Jo Dingemans
1999, Palgrave Macmillan

Textiles Now
Author: Drusilla Cole
2008, Laurence King

The Pocket Guide to Fashion PR
Author: Sophie Sheikh
2009, Preo Publishing

*Visual Merchandising: Window and In-Store Displays
for Retail*
Author: Tony Morgan
2008, Laurence King

Writing for the Fashion Business
Authors: Kristen K. Swanson & Judith C. Everett
2008, Fairchild Books

(Left to right) Katsiaryna/Shutterstock Images LLC, MUA: Claire Salter / Photographer: Sarah Jones

USEFUL WEBSITES

www.artsthread.com
Great site to see the work of fashion graduates, read practical advice guides, and check their directory of fashion colleges and universities

www.businessoffashion.com
Daily fashion news articles, interviews and features

www.canucutit.co.uk
Fashion careers advice site

www.fashioncapital.co.uk
Comprehensive information and advice site, featuring talk forums, event and competition information, practial tips and careers guidance

www.fashioncontest.com
Fashion networking site, mainly for aspiring models, photographers and designers

www.fashionunited.com
Good site for keeping up-to-date with fashion business news

www.nineteen74.com
Fashion networking site for designers, journalists, photographers, make-up artists and students

www.prospects.ac.uk
General careers advice site

www.fashion-stylist.net/blog
Fashion info site, featuring insider interviews, news and events diary

www.thefashioncareersclinic.blogspot.com
Our blog! If you've enjoyed reading this book, check this out for more careers advice and news, updated on a regular basis

www.thefashpack.onsugar.com
Regular fashion and beauty interviews, news and street style features

www.stylebubble.co.uk
Cool blog on all things fashion!

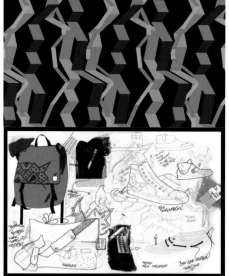

TOP: Sholto Drumlanrig
UPPER MIDDLE: Andy Thompson
LOWER MIDDLE: Stylist: Mhairi Gibb / Photographer: Gemma Booth
BOTTOM: Michele Palma

Image: Sholto Drumlanrig

CREDITS

Writing this book has been a real learning curve and wouldn't have been possible without the generosity, time and information given by a vast number of contributors. Thank you all so much for your support along the way – many of you have given your time and knowledge freely and generously, often at short notice, and it has been hugely appreciated. The book would not have been possible without you all – not only for the text content, but also for the amazing imagery and photography created by a wonderful team of photographers, stylists, models, make-up artists and hair stylists. On that note, a special mention goes to our brilliant cover illustrator, Julie Bouiguerourene. I knew as soon as I saw your website that you would do a fantastic job, and I was right – your interpretation of the brief was spot on.

Thanks to my publisher, Jenny Ross at Adelita. This project would never have seen the light of day without your support and belief in the concept. Thanks for your words of wisdom and your patience.

Lee Mitchell – layout designer extraordinaire! It looks brilliant due to your time and commitment, which I appreciate very much. You've been fantastic – thanks for being a great designer, and a true friend.

Gosh, this is like an Oscar's speech, but HUGE thanks to all of my wonderful friends and family for your support and belief that I could do it. Special thanks to Mum, Dad, Gareth, Zoe and Alan for your love and words of encouragement.

And last but not least – to my wonderful husband, Gavin – thanks for your never-ending love, support and patience. I couldn't have done it without you. All my love,TB.

p129	Image: CandyBoxPhoto/Shutterstock Images LLC
p131	Image: Katsiaryna/Shutterstock Images LLC
p132	Image: Nito/Shutterstock Images LLC
p135	Photographer: Chris Moore /
	Show production: John Walford
	Show Production: Luke Foy /
	Photographer: Christopher Dadey
p137	Show Production: Luke Foy/Photographer: Chris Moore
p138	Portrait of Luke Foy: Photographer – Will Sanders
p139	Show Production: John Walford / Show Assistant: Luke Foy/
	Photographer: Chris Moore
p140-141	All images – John Walford
p142	Show Production: Luke Foy /
	Photographer: Jose Westerman
p151	Photo of Viki Wittering: Laura Hintz, c/o Lulu Guinness
	Zoran Karapancev/Shutterstock Images LLC
	MUA: Claire Salter / Photographer: James Lightbown
p154	Image: Katsiaryna/Shutterstock Images LLC
	MUA: Claire Salter / Photographer: Sarah Jones
p153	Sholto Drumlanrig
	Andy Thompson
	Mhairi Gibb / Photographer: Gemma Booth
	Michele Palma
p157	Sholto Drumlanrig

p78	Photographer: Robert Harper /
	Hair & Make-up Artist: Claire Salter /
	Stylist & Art Direction: Naomi Mdudu
p79 (i)	Photographer – Sarah Jones /
	Make-up Artist – Claire Salter
p79 (ii)	Photographer: Jamie Nelson /
	Make-up Artist: Tomara Watkins /
	Hair Stylist: Eric R Williams / Stylist: Ope Majek
p81	Photographer: James Lightbown /
	Hair & Make-up: Claire Salter
p82	Photographer: Robert Harper/ Hair&Make-up: Claire Salter /
	Stylist & Art Direction: Naomi Mdudu
p83	Photographer: Melissa Scheetz /
	Make-up Artist: Tomara Watkins /
	Hair Stylist: Eve Whittington
p84	Photographer: Gary Steer /
	Hair & Make-up Artist: Claire Salter

CONTACTS

Gemma Booth, Photographer: www.gemmabooth.com
Julie Bouiguerourene, www.jwls.fr
Katie Burnett, Stylist www.katieburnett.co.uk
Stefano Brunesci, Photographer: www.stefanobrunesci.com
Keith Clouston, Photographer: www.keithclouston.com
Vanessa Collins, Hair & Make-up Artist: www.vanessa-collins.com
Christopher Dadey, Photographer: www.christopherdadey.com
Gregory Dean, Hair Stylist: www.gregorydean.co.uk
Polly Errington, Stylist: www.pollyerrington.co.uk
Shinya Fukami, Hair Stylist: www.shinyafukami.info
Mhairi Gibb, Stylist: www.mhairigibb.com
Alistair Guy, Photographer: www.alistairguy.com
Robert Harper, Photographer: www.robertharper.co.uk
Kate Johns, Make-up Artist: www.katejohns.com
Sarah Jones, Photographer: www.sarahjonesphotography.co.uk
Tobias Key, Photographer: www.tobiaskey.com
Alex Leonhardt, Photographer: www.ale-photo.com
James Lightbown, Photographer: www.jameslightbown.co.uk / www.cliclamode.com
Naomi Mdudu, Stylist/Art Direction: www.thefashpack.onsugar.com
Chris Moore, Photographer: www.catwalking.com
Viktoria Moskalova, Hair Stylist/Model/Stylist: www.viktoriamodesta.com
Jamie Nelson, Photographer: www.jamienelson.com
Madeleine Østlie, Stylist: www.seamlessfashion.blogspot.com
Claire Salter, Make-up Artist: www.clairesalter.co.uk
Will Sanders, Photographer: www.willsbook.com
Melissa Scheetz, Photographer: www.melissascheetz.com
Gary Steer, Photographer: www.garysteer.com
Anne Veck, Hair Stylist: www.anneveckhair.com
Tomara Watkins, Make-up Artist: www.twatkinsbeauty.com
Cat Watson, Stylist: www.cat-watson.com / www.cliclamode.com
Eve Whittington, Hair Stylist: www.evewhittington.com
Eric R Williams, Hair Stylist: www.ericrwilliams.com

EXTRA CREDITS

DESIGN CHAPTER
| p22 | Photograph of Mohsin Sajid: Sadia Rafique |

STYLING CHAPTER
p55	Photographer - Stefano Brunesci /
	Make-up Artist - Claire Salter / Hair Stylist - Anne Veck /
	Model - Rachel @ Nevs
p56	Photographer - Alex Leonhardt /
	Make-up Artist - Vanessa Collins /
	Hair Stylist - Viktoria Moskalova / Model - Belle @ D1
p57	Photographer - Stefano Brunesci /
	Make-up Artist - Claire Salter / Hair Stylist - Anne Veck /
	Model - Keeley @ Nevs
p59 (i)	Photographer: Stefano Brunesci /
	Make-up Artist: Claire Salter / Hair Stylist: Anne Veck /
	Model: Keeley @ Nevs
p59 (ii)	Photographer: Stefano Brunesci /
	Make-up Artist: Claire Salter / Hair Stylist: Anne Veck /
	Model: Rachel @ Nevs
p61	Photographer – Gemma Booth / Stylist – Mhairi Gibb /
	Photography Assistants - Alex Forsey & Katie Cox /
	Styling Assistant - Jess Runciman /
	Prop Styling -Sarah May /
	Make-up Artist - Angela Davis Deacon at Naked /
	Hair Stylist - Panos at CLM / Retouching at Core Digital
p62	Photographer – Keith Clouston / Stylist – Cat Watson
p63-64	Photographer – Gemma Booth / Stylist – Mhairi Gibb /
	Photography Assistants - Alex Forsey & Katie Cox /
	Styling Assistant - Jess Runciman /
	Prop Styling -Sarah May /
	Make-up Artist - Angela Davis Deacon at Naked /
	Hair Stylist - Panos at CLM / Retouching at Core Digital

MAKE-UP CHAPTER
p77 (i)	Photographer: Rob Harper / Make-up Artist: Claire Salter /
	Hair Stylist: Shinya Fukami / Stylist: Katie Burnett
p77 (ii)	Photographer: Tobias Key / Make-up Artist: Kate Johns /
	Model: Kayt Webster-Brown

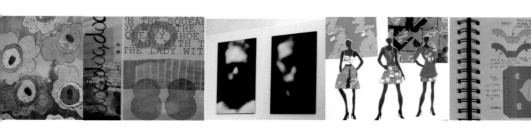